ASTRAL

A JACK DOYLE PARANORMAL MYSTERY

MARK REEDER

HANGAR 1 PUBLISHING

OTHER BOOKS BY MARK REEDER

ACKNOWLEDGMENTS

The author thanks the members of the Online Writers Workshop, a community of writers who help one another improve each other's skills, whose comments and suggestions have made this a much better book, including Robyn Wescombe, Kathryn Jankowski, Zvi Zaks, Rayne Hall, and Holly Ann Grant; and Ron Meyer, my mentor and friend who encourages me to write.

My sincerest apologies to all Seattleites for altering the fair Emerald City's neighborhoods and for creating places, people, and events out of whole cloth. This is, after all, a novel.

PROLOGUE

1

Seattle, Washington
Ferry Dock 305

Andrew Chapman kept his eyes on the bobbing ramp as he guided the SUV from the Bainbridge Ferry onto the wharf at Seattle's 305 Terminal. He knew, to the ship's crew, eager to get home to their families after the night's last docking, he was driving overcautiously. He didn't care; not with the important cargo on board.

His husband, Ray Harris, chuckled softly beside him and whispered, "Ain't they cute?"

Once on solid ground, Chapman relaxed his grip on the steering wheel and glanced in the rearview mirror at the couple's adopted Vietnamese daughters. The twin seven-year-olds were tucked under blankets among the camping supplies, their rosy cheeks and black, mop-haired heads visible alongside Bigfoot dolls purchased in Squim. This Labor Day weekend had been a three-day camping trip to the Olympic Peninsula and the Strait of Juan de Fuca. They laughingly called it Expedition Sasquatch, because both girls were hoping to spot the elusive, legendary creature.

Gina and Lena were the most important people in Chapman's life.

At thirty-four years old, he had reached the peak of his career as a neuro-linguistics researcher at the University of Washington in Seattle. His research had taken a surprising turn in the past five years, when he theorized the human brain could link directly to Earth's geomagnetic field through Schumann resonance. His *Mind Journeys* podcast on traveling the astral plane by bending Earth's magnetic field to the mind's will had catapulted him into the heady realm, where real science overlapped with the occult.

While the scientific community pooh-poohed his research and ideas, the internet made him a folk hero among tarot readers, seers, witches, and gypsy fortunetellers. Chapman's translated into he and Ray affording to live in the priciest part of Queen Anne Hill on Seattle's Puget Sound shore. But he had never considered himself truly wealthy until he and his partner had adopted the twins eighteen months ago.

Chapman stretched in the seat, felt the kinks in his lower back, and groaned. "It'll be good to get home and sleep in a real bed for a change."

Ray gave him a good-natured punch in the arm. "You getting old and soft on me, buddy?"

"Appreciative of the good things in life," Chapman countered, pointing his thumb at the back seat. "Those two in particular."

"Amen to that," Ray answered.

Theirs was the last car to disembark. Engine trouble had delayed the ferry, and it was after two in the morning. The ticket office would not reopen for another three hours, and the empty parking area beckoned them to leave.

Chapman gunned the engine through the exit and onto Alaskan Way, heading north toward home. A sharp twang reverberated through the SUV, and the black hook of a bungee cord flapped against the windshield.

Ray tapped his shoulder. "Pull over, Andy. Let me fix that before the whole load slides off the back."

Chapman hesitated. The wide street, empty of cars at this early hour, seemed as barren as a desert. The nearest streetlight sputtered, submerging the area in kaleidoscopic darkness. "I don't know. We're only a couple of miles from home. It'll hang together until we get there."

Ray laughed. "You know I'm not going to give this up. So, you might as well pull over and let me do my thing. It'll only take a sec. Promise."

A former Navy Seal who had seen tours of duty in Iraq and Afghanistan, Ray was indefatigable when he got an idea in his head. Chapman tapped the brakes and coasted onto the shoulder beneath the stuttering streetlight. "Make it quick, and don't wake the girls."

"Quiet as an ant at a picnic," Ray promised and exited the car before it rolled to a stop.

Chapman checked the girls in the back. They slept soundly. He sighed and leaned against the headrest. A metallic tap on his window drew his attention. He swiveled his head and saw through the tinted glass a man wearing a ski mask — dark eyes with slight epicanthic folds, and large pupils as if he were on meth or ecstasy. The dark muzzle of a TEC-9 pointed at Chapman's face, moving in a jerky circle.

He sat frozen, mesmerized by a flaming dragon tat on the man's gun arm. Under the streetlamp's stuttering light, intricate hues of blue, yellow, and red rippled around gaping jaws filled with rows of sharp teeth and two fangs. The neuroscientist part of his mind explained his fascination as a fear response of the amygdala using small details as a means to regulate his emotions so he didn't freeze in terror.

The gangbanger didn't give a crap about science. He smashed the window with the barrel of the machine pistol, showering Chapman with fragments of glass.

Chapman hurriedly unfastened his seatbelt. Glancing once at the twins suddenly awake, hunkered under their blankets to stay invisible, he opened the door and nearly fell out of the car in his haste to comply with the carjacker.

His heart raced. His movements felt clumsy, and it seemed to him he wasn't going anywhere at all. The gangbanger grabbed his coat and shoved him against the car. Legs rubbery and chest burning, Chapman collapsed against the frame. His only thoughts were about the girls, and he hoped this was nothing more than a robbery.

Looking up across the roof of the SUV, he saw Ray, arms spread, hands gripping the roof rack. A second robber held a TEC-9 inches from his temple. Ray had a mocking smile on his face, and his blue eyes flicked from Chapman to the second robber and back to the firearm with a metronomic quality as if gauging the right time to fight back.

Chapman knew that look, knew the anger and prowess it held in check, had seen it explode in lightning-fast movements at the self-defense gym where Ray taught. *No!* He pleaded with his eyes, hoping his thoughts penetrated Ray's bravado. *Let them have the car and money. We'll take the girls and walk home.*

In the next instant, Ray's hand flicked out in a casual gesture, knocking the machine pistol aside as if batting at a mosquito. His other hand whipped at the robber's throat, fingers clawed to crush the larynx. The blow never reached its target. The gun beside Chapman's head roared, the staccato thunder deafening him. Ray's head exploded in a pink mist.

The gun kept firing indiscriminately. The SUV's rear windows exploded. The two girls sat up, dark eyes wide with terror. Their angelic faces disappeared behind the rain of shattered glass. Chapman whirled to stop the firing. Something struck him in the back of the head. Burning flame lanced through him, and darkness mercifully followed.

2

Seattle
Harborview Medical Center

"He's very handsome," the young nurse said, looking down at the middle-aged man on the gurney.

The patient was handsome. Greek god profile, aquiline nose, high cheekbones, and prominent cleft chin. A wisp of black hair stuck out from under the white gauze swathing his head.

She read the name on the chart. "Andrew Chapman." She clucked her tongue in pity. "What a tragedy. To lose your family..."

"Shush," Geneva Bowen said, cutting her off with an indulgent smile.

Geneva was the senior trauma nurse at Seattle's prestigious Harborview Medical Center and had assigned herself and the newbie to transfer Mr. Andrew Chapman from the ER to the ICU. She smiled sadly at the patient lying motionless on the white hospital linen with an IV in his left arm dripping fluids into a vein. A ventilator on a separate cart steadily hummed air into and out of his lungs. "Coma patients can hear you," she said softly.

"That's not true," the young woman scoffed. This was only her second week out of nursing school, and she was new to the ER.

The veteran nurse stared at her with a look of pity and understanding until she looked down in confusion. Geneva squeezed her arm compassionately. "There's so much more that happens in healing than any textbook can teach you. Best always to believe the patient is listening."

Geneva Bowen was big, black, and beautiful. Her hair was dyed blond and cut close to her scalp in tiny curls. Those who worked with her often commented with amazement how her dark brown eyes always danced with laughter, and she had a wide uncomplaining grin for everyone. No patient or staff member ever felt anything but happy when around her. She'd joined Harborview Medical Center thirty-five years ago, straight out of nursing school. Never married, she explained to everyone who asked why that she had no time for a husband. Her patients were her children.

She smiled, her turquoise lips accenting her rouged face and plucked eyebrows. "You're going to learn stuff you thought couldn't possibly be true. You'll change a lot in just a year. You'll see."

Easing the gurney next to the wall of the ICU, while the nurses inside finished preparing a space for their newest patient, Geneva spoke in a whisper only the new nurse could hear. "Besides, would you want to know your husband and daughters were butchered in some kind of botched gang initiation?"

"How do you know what happened, Geneva?"

Geneva's smile tightened. She felt a frown, as well as the sadness that would surely follow it, building inside her skull, the memory of her murdered niece bellowing to be heard over the thin veneer of happiness she showed the world. *Don't go there!* she ordered herself and kept the sorrow away from her face with sheer will. "My brother is a detective with the Seattle police. He called me when he heard the only survivor was headed here."

The young nurse looked at the victim's face. A trickle of blood seeped from the head bandages. She removed a wipe from the pack at her waist and carefully dabbed it away. "What's going to happen to him? Doctor Jones said he'd never wake up, and even if he does, there's too much damage. He'll be a vegetable for the rest of his life."

Geneva scowled at the thought. "He's Doctor Andrew Chapman. His podcast, *Mind Journeys on the Astral Plane*, has the most listeners in the country." When the young woman shook her head, she added, "He has lots of money. I'm sure his relatives will take care of the poor dear."

She laid her hand against Chapman's cheek and brushed away the tears running down it. *How could he be crying if he's in a persistent vegetative state?* She said nothing to the new nurse.

3

Seattle
Greenbrier Nursing Home
One Year Later

Geneva Bowen looked at her watch. It was a little after 8:30, which explained why she was tired. Her shift at the hospital had been particularly tough. Late in the afternoon, a pile-up on the I-5 near Freeway Park had sent twelve cases to Harborview Medical Center. She had almost decided to go home first before visiting Andrew Chapman.

For the last nine months, every evening after leaving work, Geneva had stopped by the Greenbrier Nursing Home, a high-end, long-term care spa for the dying. She thought everybody should have the chance to let go of life comfortably. But in thirty-six years of work at Harborview's ER trauma center, she had seen enough of dying to know many would never get the chance to go peacefully, surrounded by loved ones. Bullets, knives, car accidents, poison, and poverty worsened the odds in brutality's favor.

Geneva pulled into her usual parking space near the nursing home's front entrance but did not get out of her car right away.

Unexpectedly, the face of her beautiful niece surfaced in her thoughts. Two years ago, Andrea had been celebrating her sixteenth birthday at the mall, a mile from her home in Auburn. One moment, an innocent bystander laughing with friends; the next, a victim of a drive by shooting. Earlier that day, Andrea had told everyone her birthday wish was to become a nurse, just like her aunt. Much later after the funeral, Geneva's detective brother told her the I-5 Dragon Triad was responsible, though no one could prove it.

Maybe that's why Andrew Chapman's situation hit me so hard. He's a victim of those triad animals just like Andrea. Their names are even similar.

Carefully putting the painful memory away in its special mental compartment, Geneva put on her best smile and sailed through the nursing home's front entrance the way she always did, full of happiness. Greenbrier was a way station for the dying, but that didn't mean it had to have the ambience of a tomb. She thought everyone deserved a good old-fashioned Irish wake sendoff. After nine months, the staff appreciated her joy.

"How's my favorite patient this evening, Clara?" she asked, stopping at the front desk to chat with the evening duty nurse.

The older woman looked up from the computer screen. "Mr. Chapman doesn't change, Geneva. He's steady as a rock. If I didn't know better, I'd say he'd wake up tomorrow morning as good as ever."

Geneva bit her lip. She didn't like it when the medical staff treated Andrew Chapman as if he should already be dead. She had researched his life, especially his neuroscience work correlating the brain, mind, and consciousness. She was convinced his soul lived on within his body, alive and desperate to be reunited with the world.

Ever since he'd rolled into the ER at Harborview a year ago, she had seen it as her job to help him get well and help him with whatever plans he had once he woke up. That was why she spent every evening at Greenbrier before going home to her two-bedroom condo on the backside of Capitol Hill and her fifteen-year-old Maine Coon cat, Onyx.

She started down the corridor to Chapman's first-floor room, when the night nurse called out, "He has visitors."

"Who?" Geneva asked, suddenly on guard. In nine months, no one had once stopped by to see Chapman, not even his so-called cousins.

"Relatives," the nurse answered with such disdain Geneva wanted to hurry to the room to protect her patient. Instead, she walked back to the desk.

"What do those ghouls want?"

Clara leaned forward and whispered, "I overheard them talking about asking a judge to have Chapman removed from life support so he could die with dignity."

Geneva's hand flew to her mouth. "Is he...?" She swallowed her fear and glared toward Chapman's room.

Clara shook her head. "The judge hasn't ruled yet. You still have time to say goodbye."

Geneva hurried down the hall, her mind churning with ideas of how to stop the execution, for she knew it would be an execution. And for what? Money! She fumed at the image of the so-called family standing before the judge, faking compassion for their cousin; they only wanted his multimillion-dollar estate.

The door to Chapman's room stood wide open, and Geneva heard arguing as she approached. A loud man urged the family not to wait for the judge's decision and demanded they remove Chapman from life support right now.

Peering around the doorjamb, she saw seven people crowded around the bed. The ventilator whispered smoothly up and down, pushing air into Chapman's lungs, while the monitor above the bed displayed his blood pressure at 100 over 60, blood-oxygen level at 97 percent, and his pulse at 50. At the head of the bed hummed an EEG machine the family had him hooked up to as a means of showing whether Chapman was in a coma or a persistent vegetative state. The graph was flat.

Geneva didn't believe it. Even from this distance, she could see tears on his cheeks. The man's brain must be working.

The family noticed her at the door, and the arguing ceased. The largest of the cousins, a burly man in his fifties, pushed through the others and stood in front of her, fists clenched. "Family only," he grated.

Geneva didn't flinch. She jabbed a finger at the bedridden figure. "Andrew is alive. Leave him alone."

"Get out!" the man shouted.

"I'm not afraid of you," she said, muscles along her jaw trembling. "I'll call security. I'll—"

"We're family, and you ain't. Get the hell out before I call security on you." He slammed the door in her face.

"Ghouls," Geneva muttered.

4

Greenbrier Nursing Home

Geneva Bowen left but didn't go far. She sat at the end of the hall on a plush green couch gazing out an open window. Soft blue twilight gleamed through the thicket of cedar trees and butterscotch pines surrounding the nursing home. The fragrant smells combined with the quiet chittering of insects were meant to soothe the nerves of the old and dying as well as relatives.

Geneva wasn't soothed. Her heart beat savagely in her large bosomed against the unjust whimsy of a world that would leave a fine man like Andrew Chapman at the unmerciful hands of gold-digging cousins. It chafed that though she was a nurse and had only Chapman's interests at heart, she wasn't family. She was an outsider. The cousins had all the power.

But Geneva wasn't ready to give up. She concentrated her mind, using techniques she had gleaned from listening to Chapman's podcasts on consciousness and the astral plane, and willed the cousins to leave him untouched.

Twenty minutes later, they filed out of the room, grumbling

among themselves. The big guy clenched a fist and hissed at the others, "We shoulda just done it. No one would have said a thing."

A short fat woman with red-dyed hair spotted Geneva at the end of the hall and screamed at him to be quiet. They ignored her and hurried toward the front entrance.

Once they left the building, she slipped into the room.

Andrew Chapman lay unmoving on the hospital bed his face drawn and wrinkled. The color in his cheeks was as pale as the sheets covering him. In the last nine months, his body had withered into a husk of its former muscular self.

She paid scant attention to the machines keeping him alive but went over to his bedside and brushed his cheek with long, thick fingers. The dark red nails contrasted sharply with Chapman's pallor. She felt the tears and checked the EEG machine. The readout stayed flat.

The gauze surrounding his head had long been removed, and unruly black hair draped across the pillow in tangles. Taking a brush from her purse, Geneva combed his hair, talking to him all the time in the low, melodious, soft voice she used to soothe the patients of Harborview Medical Center's ER. "I read online you were nominated for a Nobel Prize for your work on brain waves and electromagnetic radiation. I'm sure you would have won, except for what happened to your family."

Geneva finished unknotting the last of the tangles then arranged the sheet and blanket covering him and plumped the pillow beneath his head. "I know you're in there, Mr. Chapman. You just need the right motivation to free yourself, and I have the right thing with me," she whispered.

Settling her Rubenesque figure into the nearest chair, Geneva pulled a manila folder out of a large handbag. The seal of the Seattle Police Department adorned the cover. "My brother is a cop, and he got me the official report on the investigation into your family's murder."

She began reading to Chapman about how the police investigation had stalled. "A detective... Umm... his name is Jack Doyle... He's convinced the I-5 Dragon Triad murdered your husband and adopted daughters. He can't prove it though. I bet you could, if you would only wake up."

Geneva looked up from the folder. "You have to wake up, Andrew. If you don't, those gangbangers are going to get away with murder." She bit her lip. "Just like they did with Andrea... my niece."

Tears glimmered on Chapman's cheeks.

Geneva wrung the report in her hands. She slid the chair closer. Her voice became a murmur of hope. "I know you can hear me, Andrew. The Chinese gang responsible for the deaths of your husband and your daughters is still out there hurting others." More tears slipped out of Andrew's eyes. She squeezed his hand. "You have to wake up, or else they'll never pay for what they did to you. And if you don't hurry, your family is going to pull the plug on the machines. You have to do something to show them you're alive."

Geneva's turquoise lips parted in a gasp as Chapman's hand returned the pressure.

She gripped his fingers harder and leaned in until her lips were inches from his ear. "We have to wake you up," she pleaded. Laying his hand gently on the bed, she smoothed the already faultless covers. She read to him all the information in the report on the I-5 Dragons, laying out who they were and where they could be found.

The room was deathly still. Not even the curtains in the open window shrugged from the breeze. Chapman's cadaver-like face remained placid as she spoke. No sound issued from his silent lips. Geneva heard only the quiet *whish-whish* of the ventilator and the soft beep of his pulse from the monitor.

Even as her rational mind told her Chapman couldn't do anything about the information she gave him, she refused to stop. She paused after several minutes, looked up from the file, and gasped again. Chapman's eyelids twitched.

She continued reading, the injustice of his situation imbuing her voice with passion. Chapman's eyes fluttered with each word she spoke, and his face flushed with what she thought must be righteous anger, confirming her suspicion that the soul and personality of Andrew Chapman lurked somewhere deep inside his brain, eager to get free.

As a Christian, Geneva felt her maternal love swell at the thought and drew closer to him. She closed the cover on the report, took Chapman's skeletal hand between both of hers, and prayed aloud from Leviticus 24:18-22. "If anyone injures his neighbor, as he has done it shall be done to him, fracture for fracture, eye for eye, tooth for tooth. Whatever injury he has given a person shall be given to him. Whoever kills an animal shall make it good, and whoever kills a person shall be put to death. You shall have the same rule for the sojourner and for the native, for I am the Lord your God.'"

She took in a deep breath and squeezed his hands in hers. "Please wake up, Mr. Chapman. You have to stop these evil men."

At first, the room's silence pushed at Geneva with a reassuring gentleness. Then, a curious thing happened that gave her Christian belief hope and terrified her at the same time. The lights dimmed. The ventilator continued to purr but at much longer intervals now, as though Chapman was taking deep breaths. The EEG machine beeped madly, and the readout scribbled wildly across the screen. On the monitor, his blood pressure shot up and his heartbeat sped to over 100 beats per minute.

More surprising, none of the alarms that should have erupted at the rocketing heartbeat and blood pressure made a sound, as if turned off.

Geneva let go of Chapman's hand and sat frozen in her chair. Her eyes darted from one machine to another, and she almost missed the saintly transformation of the bedridden soul in front of her. A pale, unearthly aura in the form of Chapman rose out of his emaciated body. It grew into the embodiment of his healthy self before the shooting. It hovered above the bed, staring at her, before leaving in a whirl of wind through the open window.

Shivering in fright and ecstasy, Geneva slid from the chair to her knees and wept. Hands clasped on the bed, she prayed to God, to heaven, to the Earth. And in case the Christian god was not enough, Geneva prayed to every deity she could name to help Andrew Chapman, wherever he was and whatever he was about.

PART I

CHINATOWN

5

Seattle, Washington
Ornate Grand Pavilion
Hing Hay Park, Chinatown

I love Seattle at night in August. It smells like a city on the edge of tomorrow. The air is crisp with green growing things, restaurants permeate the surroundings with tempting cosmopolitan aromas, and a mix of industry and car exhaust underlies everything living with the unscrubbed odor of progress.

At night, the streets are a wash of neon-lit storefronts advertising the flashy brilliance of a brassy destiny. From its founding in 1851, Seattle has been a jumping-off point for history. The Alaskan gold rush, the aerospace industry, tech, e-commerce, and gay rights have made the city a rambunctious, hi-rev environment of the future.

Whatever the reason, I love this town in summer, when I can forget the winter rains and endless steel-gray clouds enfolding the Pacific Northwest's Emerald City in a damp chill and concentrate on the beauty that attracts people from across the world to its fair environs.

The Hing Hay Grand Pavilion, in the heart of Chinatown, is one such attraction. It's painted in garish colors. Square, red columns support a steep, *golden, tiled roof. Tiny, gilded dragon, monkey, bird, and lion gargoyles peer down at the crowds from the corners. Like a Buddhist temple, it's open on all sides.*

I spend a decent amount of time in Chinatown, since it's part of the West Precinct, where I work. But my presence could also be attributed to my Punjabi grandparents, who settled here after Partition in 1947 forced them out of Pakistan and India. On the other side of my family, I have an Irish great uncle killed in Dublin's 1916 Easter uprising. A lot of tragic history in my family. Maybe that's why I became a cop.

Heavy kliegs lit up Chinatown's Grand Pavilion in a barrage of light. It looked like a set on *America's Greatest Mysteries*. I flashed my detective badge, and the uniformed officer lifted the bright yellow tape so I didn't have to stoop to enter the crime scene. I'm not tall, a bit under six feet, and healthy for a guy who's been on the donut diet for fourteen years. Not really. Risperdal played havoc with my metabolism until I figured out I had to give up alcohol and sugar. Still, I prefer walking upright and not bent over like some ape.

The young woman cop was Chinese American. She had that easygoing way about her that second-generation Asian Americans have from growing up on American television and learning not to fear authority. She was tall and wore her bulletproof vest like it was part of her.

I squinted at the woman's nametag: *Liu.* I guessed her parents came from the north, so I said in Mandarin, "What's your take on this, Officer Liu?" I learned early as a detective to get the impression of the cops who arrived first on the scene.

"Sandra," she answered instead and held out her hand.

"Jack Doyle," I said. We shook while my eyes darted over her like a bird looking for food. The rapid eye movement puts some people off. I can't help it.

"You okay?" she asked, nodding toward my face. "Your eyes."

I have TD — tardive dyskinesia. It causes stiff, jerky movements I can't control. It's a side effect of my medication. I wasn't telling, though. If anyone in the squad found out I was on a low dose of Risperdal, I'd be out of a job faster than Usain Bolt from the starting blocks. I like being a detective, and I'm a damn good one. I approach a case as if putting together a jigsaw puzzle with the key pieces scattered on the floor and in other rooms. Besides, TD doesn't affect my mind or my hands... yet.

"Habit," I said. "I meet someone new, and I check them out. So, what do we have?"

Sandra Liu frowned and replied, "The murder's brutal. The killer had a lot of personal rage against the skel."

"Skel?"

"Willie Fong."

"Shit!" I cursed silently in five more languages. My eyes swept the area. Chinatown was home to a multitude of tongs and the I-5 Dragon Triad. The last thing Seattle needed was a war between the two.

6

Ornate Grand Pavilion
Hing Hay Park

E *ncyclopedia Britannica defines a Tong War as 'any of several feuds carried on in US cities between gangs of Chinese immigrants or their descendants. These gang wars spanned a 70-year period beginning in the 1850s and continued until the 1920s. The term* tong *came to be used by the white population in the 1880s, usually to refer to fraternal organizations involved in illegal activities, such as opium trade or gambling.'*

The real history is a lot more complicated. Chinese immigrants faced dangers that would make the average white person forget about coming to the United States. Preyed upon by lawless members of their own society, as well as enduring discrimination and violence by whites, they banded together in tongs for protection. Originally, these secret societies were specialized groups of merchants, craftsmen, and tradespeople. But criminals organized too, specializing in opium, prostitution, gambling, and the protection racket.

Nowadays, people confuse tongs with the triads — vicious organized crime groups from Hong Kong, Macau, and Taiwan. Here in Seattle, the American-Chinese community prefers the traditional name, tong, *which* means 'hall' or 'meeting place.' The older community looks down on the I-5 Dragon Triad as interlopers with no respect.

"Strange that anyone would run into the Grand Pavilion for protection unless chased by demons, Jack."

I would have recognized the nasally voice of Seattle's Chief medical examiner, Dr. Melvin Hagler, across Hing Hay Park on a Monday afternoon, crowded with loud workers and even louder tourists sharing their lunch hour at Seattle's historic Chinatown gate. At midnight, it was like a bullhorn announcing his presence.

"Mel," I said, not unfriendlily but not warmly either. Mel Hagler stole the woman I thought I was going to marry. Or maybe she chose him over me. Either way, we weren't friends. Not enemies either. We were caught in that no-man's-land, where the saying "bros before hos" didn't operate.

Hagler was straddling the victim, taking a selfie for his collection of famous Seattle murders, no doubt. The klieg lights were so bright, he didn't need the flash. They were necessary though. The streetlights in the area had exploded, as if a surge of electricity shot through them like in a 1950s B-horror flick.

In fact, the whole scene was surreal, straight out of detective film noir. I've read Hammett, Spillane, Chandler, Cornwell, Leonard — you name him or her. I'm an avid fan of the genre. I've also seen Bogart's *The Maltese Falcon* a dozen times, but I had never seen anything as gruesome as Willie Fong's murder. The only way Sandra Liu knew who the broken bones, battered face, and caved-in skull belonged to was through ID.

"Cause of death?" I asked.

Hagler rolled his eyes. "Seriously? You look at that body and wonder what the cause of death is?"

"Mel, Willie Fong was the number-one enforcer for the I-5 Dragons. What are the chances someone beat him this way unless they rendered him helpless first?"

"Or they surprised him."

I shook my head. "Not Willie. He was a legend. Story goes, a rival triad in San Francisco put a contract on him. He arrived at their headquarters on Grant Avenue, killed both hitmen before they left the building, then negotiated peace with the triad leadership."

"Stories," Hagler scoffed.

"Yeah, stories. Even so, Willie was one of a kind. Do me a favor. Be extra careful with your autopsy. Let me know if he was incapacitated first."

"Anything particular I should look for?"

I smiled. "Lead poisoning."

Hagler groaned, shook his head, and turned back to the vic. He waited until I turned away and tossed over his shoulder, "Hey, Doyle. Cassie says hello."

My stomach knotted, and I took a long breath to play out the fantasy of drawing my service weapon and shooting Hagler in the balls. Cassandra O'Neill was the one who got away. I couldn't stop myself from asking, "How is she?"

"Pregnant. Twins again."

"You know they have pills that stop that kind of shit."

"We're Catholic."

"Cut it off."

"You're just jealous," Hagler said.

I gave him my best Irish smile, which I get from my dad's side of the family. "The word's envious. If I were jealous, I'd have killed you ten years ago before you asked her to marry you."

I left him wondering if I was serious. Truth be told, I wasn't sure myself.

7

Seattle Police Department
West Precinct

The West Precinct includes the port of Seattle and is the busiest in the city, busier than Chinatown. It also has more Asian-American cops than any other precinct. It even has a Nepalese traffic warden. So far, she's given me half a dozen tickets. They're gathering creases in my car's glove box. The next step would be a warrant for my arrest, and I'm hoping she doesn't disappoint me.

I'm quirky this way; at least the shrink I see once a month tells me so. I think it's another side effect of the Risperdal. Then again, I've been on it since six, and thirty years later, it's part of who I am now as a detective with Seattle's CID — the Criminal Investigative Division. Detectives with CID are responsible for investigating the crimes at the Port of Seattle. CID grabbed me out of the academy because I speak a lot of languages. I never forget a word I hear. It's a gift, and one of the symptoms the medication treats.

. . .

I stood by my desk with a mountain of paper on it, mostly low-level stuff — a stolen car, a jewelry heist on the Gold Coast (that's what I call the neighborhood on the east shore of Puget Sound, where the one-percenters live), and a couple of warrants for felony menacing . I wasn't looking at any of those. I listened to the large clock counting off the seconds as it ticked past 9:15. A small blackboard hung below it, like one of those in a factory saying *this many days with no workplace accidents*. Only this one read *No homicides*.

The number had been 343. Someone had already erased it after last night's killing and scrawled a big zero with a line through it. The new number didn't help me any. Every day the number had gone up the past year reminded me I still hadn't solved the biggest case on my desk — the triple homicide near the ferry terminal from last year. The lone survivor was in a coma at a nursing home. He was never expected to awaken, and even if he did, he was a vegetable.

Yeah, I'm not all that PC.

Because the Ferry system was part of the Port of Seattle, the Criminal Investigations Division got the call, and I got the case.

"Doyle! In my office," Malvern shouted. The squad room went still. Even the ticking clock paused under his booming voice.

The other officers looked at me with a what-did-you-do-now? expression. It wasn't unusual. I bent the rules at least once a month, never enough to get me suspended, if you discount the medication. I waved at the captain.

He waved back, a vine of red licorice in his hand. He chewed the candy to keep from smoking. "Now," he growled, shaking his fist for emphasis.

Captain Wes Malvern was three months from retirement. And for the last six months, he'd been wearing his captain's uniform on the job every day because he believed it brought him luck. For what, no one knew. He rarely left the office, and it wasn't as if some *Terminator* character would burst in here and gun everyone down.

I went to close the door, and Malvern shook his head. "It's not that kind of talk." He waited until I sat down. "Willie Fong." It was an order.

"Let someone else take it. CID has me working the ferry terminal homicides." The murder of a family — two Vietnamese kids; and the husband was a high-profile case, especially for the gay community in Seattle, since the lone survivor was Andrew Chapman. Lots of money and a celebrity neuroscientist to boot.

Malvern frowned, which was his way of saying "No way," then said, "No other detective in the precinct is fluent in both Cantonese and Mandarin. Besides, Bucktooth Lo requested you."

"He would," I responded too quickly.

Malvern's eyes narrowed beneath his bald, black head and furrowed brow. "Do you owe him or something?"

If he only knew. I shook my head. "It's all squared up."

"How's the ferry terminal murder going?"

I shrugged. It was going nowhere.

"I read your report. It's going nowhere," Malvern said, a large bite of licorice disappearing into his wide mouth. "The only witness, one of the ferry hands driving home, saw two men fleeing the scene of the crime. He pointed out some wannabe gang member of the I-5 Dragons."

"The guy was half baked. He picked the mayor out of a photo array as the shooter."

Malvern choked. "You put her honor in a photo array?" he spluttered once he stopped coughing.

I grinned; Malvern glared. Finally, he said in as near to normal a voice as possible, "Could Willie Fong be payback?"

"Don't see how. The husband's still in a coma."

"What about the family?"

I snorted. "They all have alibis, and Tech found no references in emails or texts to anyone wanting Fong dead. Besides, they're too busy squabbling over the estate and can't wait for Chapman to kick the bucket so they can inherit it."

"Rival gang," Malvern suggested, reaching into his desk for another piece of candy. "The I-5 Dragons are rocking the boat with the murder at the terminal. Maybe the tongs want to send a message."

"Maybe," I said carefully. It could be why Bucktooth Lo asked for me personally. The I-5 Dragon Triad had solidified their control along the I-5 corridor from Vancouver, British Columbia to Tijuana, Mexico and were now muscling in on some of the traditional, older Seattle tong territories. "But it doesn't fit their style."

"Maybe it's worth checking out," Malvern said softly in his that's-an-order-and-you're-dismissed voice. I got up, and he said, "You been home yet since midnight?"

I shook my head.

"Go home. Have breakfast with your rich girlfriend. Then get your ass over to Lo's. I'm sure he's expecting you."

"Yes, boss."

But I'd already decided Bucktooth Lo had better be my next stop. The old Chinese tong leader was a stickler for protocol, and a summons from him commanded the same respectful reaction as a call from POTUS.

8

Good Luck Noodle House

The Good Luck Noodle House on Canton Alley South is the home of the Good Luck Tong, a benevolent Chinese association whose main place of business is Seattle. They have branches up and down the west coast and in Hawaii. The tongs have been in Seattle for as long as the Chinese, for 160 years, longer than most Norwegians, Swedes, and Finns.

The noodle shop is also where Bucktooth Lo can be found at any time of day or night. He owns a small apartment above the restaurant. Lo has a reputation for being a kind grandfather who helps out business owners from time to time. In reality, he is the godfather of the Seattle tongs and the city's premier information broker. He knows everything going on in the Chinese community.

I wasn't surprised he asked for me. We go back to my days as a rookie detective. I saved his nephew when the kid got into trouble with another tong. Lo paid off my gambling debts. Chinese call it guanxi — having a strong personal relationship with someone that involves moral obligations and exchanging favors. I think of our relationship as agents in a spy game; we walk a fine line between law and order.

. . .

The Good Luck Noodle Shop was a typical Chinese diner with booths along the windows and four-tops scattered around the rest of the room, straining the legal seating capacity for a restaurant this small. A pair of swinging metal doors with porthole windows separated the kitchen from the front. Black-ink calligraphy on delicate rice paper hung from four interior pillars holding up the building's second and third stories. The regulars probably thought they were cheap knockoffs of ancient masters. But I knew they were collector items Lo had purchased over the years. He hid them in plain sight.

Lo's office was an eight-person booth tucked in the back of the shop away from the windows and safe from prying eyes. I had never seen anyone else sit there. Even when the place was jumping on a Friday night and Lo wasn't around, the booth remained empty. This early in the morning, a few regulars sat in a couple of booths. They paid no attention to the old man sitting in back with the wispy goatee and a prominent gold front tooth.

When I walked up, Lo was studying the ancient Chinese game of go, the white and black pebbles laid out on a traditional wooden board divided by black lines into 361 equal squares. The game dated back to the Zhou dynasty 2,500 years ago and was once considered an essential skill by Chinese scholars. Legend said Sun Tzu played this game while writing *The Art of War*.

"You preparing to fight, Uncle Lo?" I asked in Cantonese, using the polite form of address.

He smiled, pleased with the traditional courtesy, something Asian millennials were quickly discarding for the easy way of American English. Some didn't even bother to learn Mandarin or Cantonese.

"No war, Jack," he answered without taking his eyes from the game. He motioned me to sit, and I slid onto the red faux leather bench across from him. The table was immaculate, though the Formica was chipped on the edges. The pleasant fragrance of jasmine tea wafted from delicate porcelain teacups.

I should have waited for him to take a sip. It's a face thing. By reaching for my cup first, I showed him my impatience. But it had been a long night; the only suspect from last year's triple homicide lay on Hagler's autopsy table, and I wanted to get home to my girlfriend.

I set the cup down softly. The porcelain, like the calligraphy, belonged in a museum. "The I-5 Dragon Triad doesn't play by the rules the way the older tongs do," I reminded the old man. "A lot of people in the Asian community want them out of here."

Uncle Lo settled back against the cushions. With his wispy goatee, brocaded robe, and jeweled hat, he was the perfect image of a nine-teenth-century merchant negotiating a deal. He eyed me between sips of tea. Shaking his head, he said calmly, "Everything's quiet now. Everyone's making money."

"Fortune passes everywhere," I said without irony.

"Indeed. It is why I want you to find the killer as quickly as possible. As you Americans quaintly put it, 'No one wants to rock the boat,' and this murder is bad for business."

"You Americans" was laughable. Uncle Lo played the role of an immigrant just off the boat. In reality, Charles 'Bucktooth' Lo had been born in Philadelphia at the end of World War II, the third son of a banker. He headed west to San Francisco during the "Summer of Love" and lived in Haight-Ashbury for a year, where he quickly discovered the safe money wasn't in growing and distributing weed, hashish, and tiny blue mushrooms, but in providing the means for enjoying their hallucinogenic effects. By the end of the 1970s, he owned smoke shops up and down the West Coast and moved to Seat-tle, where he rode the crest of the tech boom, putting his profits into Microsoft and Apple. I asked him once why he hadn't also invested in Google and Amazon. He answered sagely, "A man should never be greedy. It leads to bad decisions."

Lo smiled, his prominent gold front tooth gleaming under the overhead fluorescent lighting. "If you want to know who killed Willie Fong, talk to Auntie Toy. She has an interesting theory," he said by way of not changing the topic.

Auntie Toy was a legend in Seattle. She had started off life as a prostitute, became a madam, and now was in demand as a sooth-sayer, providing fortunes from a bench inside the Hing Hay Park pavilion to anyone who asked. She didn't discriminate. Her uncanny ability to glimpse the future had turned her into a Seattle institution, and though she had no license to ply her soothsayer abilities, no cop would dare arrest her. One made the mistake in 1983. While she spent the night in jail, the worst mass killing in Seattle history happened. Since then, no cop would take the chance on history repeating itself.

I studied the old man, whose left hand pulled at his wispy beard as if parodying a Chinese caricature of the benevolent elder. Lo had a dozen psychics and fortunetellers on speed dial, or would have if he trusted cell phones. He was old-school, and information was passed along in person or in coded messages on rice paper that could be burned. As I said, nineteenth century. It was also the reason the Seattle Police Department and the King County DA never had any evidence to arrest him.

I shook my head. "Don't have time for superstitious nonsense, Uncle Lo."

"You really should speak with her, Jack. She knows something."

"What did she tell you?"

"The killer is a ghost."

I sighed. The last thing I needed was to bring to the precinct a theory of ghostly apparitions killing triads. "I'll pass. I'll take an order of dim sum to go." I rarely asked for food here, not wanting to strain the feathery bonds of our relationship. But I hadn't eaten since 8:00 last night, and tea didn't settle the rumble in my stomach.

The food appeared immediately, which meant Uncle Lo knew I hadn't eaten breakfast before I walked into the noodle shop. I didn't offer to pay, because he wouldn't have accepted it.

I got into my car, ready to go home, but a call determined a different direction.

9

Harborview Medical Center
Seattle and King County ME's office

T he *Seattle and King County Medical Examiner's office is located on the second floor of the Harborview Medical Center. Its mission is to 'investigate sudden, unexpected, and unnatural deaths in King County with the highest level of professionalism, compassion, and efficiency, and to provide a resource for improving the health and safety of the community consistent with the general mission of public health.' It says so right on its website.*

As chief medical examiner, Dr. Melvin Hagler runs a tight ship. And yeah, I'm not fond of the son of a bitch, because of what happened with Cassandra, but he's good at his job and never gives me bad information.

Pulling into the hospital's parking garage, I found an open spot on the first floor. The sign on the wall said, 'Hearses Only.' I ignored it. I had larger concerns, mainly hoping Hagler lived up to the ME's mission statement and gave me a clue leading to the idiot who killed Willie Fong before a war started. The last time the Asian gangs went after each other, thirteen civilians were killed. Granted, it happened in another century, but every cop in Chinatown knew the history, and none wanted to see it repeat.

I took the stairs — part of my staying-in-shape regimen. Also, I didn't care for elevators. The Risperdal was supposed to alleviate feelings of paranoia caused by being trapped in a small cage with ten other people and wanting to shoot my way free. It didn't always help, so I found it healthy for all concerned to jog up flights of stairs.

The ME's front office was deserted, which was unusual. After news of a homicide leaked, reporters and bloggers usually flocked here to get the latest. Angela Turkel sat behind the reception desk reading something on her phone. We're old friends and even went on a couple of dates.

"Press is down in the lobby. Dr. Hagler doesn't want anyone disturbing his autopsy," she said, answering my unasked question without looking up from the tiny screen. She waved a hand at the inner sanctum. "He's expecting you."

The autopsy room was chilly, but Hagler stood in shirtsleeves and gown doing the final stitching of Willie Fong's chest. He started right in without any of his usual dawdling preliminaries, which he knew bothered the hell out of me but did anyway. The fact he didn't torture me made me wonder what else was going on.

"No defensive wounds; no skin under the fingernails. Nothing left behind by the attacker," Hagler stated from the official report he had dictated.

I jerked as if slapped upside the head. "You called me down here for nothing?"

Hagler shook his head and looked up from the cadaver. His eyes were red from crying.

"What's going on, Mel?" I asked softly.

"Think I can crash at your place? Cassie wants a separation." The words came out strangled.

I didn't know how to respond. I felt a bit giddy over the prospect of Cassandra being available. On the other hand, I was in a serious relationship with Pamela. *If it's so serious, why are you thinking about*

Cassandra? the evil voice of my twin soul asked. Yeah, growing up half Punjabi and half Irish, you tend to be a bit schizoid.

"Kind of sudden, isn't it?" I asked, shoving the distracting thought aside. "Last night, she's pregnant, and everything's good."

Hagler smiled, but his lips thinned as if drawn upwards against their will by rubber bands. "Cassie wants an abortion.... Doesn't want any more kids."

The pain in Hagler's face wasn't just about the separation. A strict Catholic, he was against abortion.

"What else can you tell me about Fong's killing?" I asked, trying to get his mind into the game and my own thoughts off Cassandra. She and I had met just after I made detective. The whirlwind romance lasted a year, and we were — at least I thought we were — moving in together. It ended with a marriage proposal. I had the ring in my sports coat pocket, all set to bend my knee and slip it on her finger, when she turned me down without any explanation. I moved out and left the sports coat behind. I took the ring with me, hocked it, and ran up a lot of gambling debt.

Hagler pulled it together. "Well, the most curious thing is, the body was completely drained of blood."

"And you didn't lead with that?" I said more forcefully than I intended.

"Sorry, other things, you know."

I did know. Thoughts of Cassandra still played tag on the edge of my consciousness. Ruthlessly, I quashed rekindled hopes I had believed long dead by staring at Willie Fong's battered body. "So, was it postmortem or what?"

"Done first. It's what killed him. He was beaten afterwards."

"So, a crime of rage."

"I'd say so, but I'm just an ME. You're the detective looking for motive."

"Who would be able to drain his blood?" I asked.

"Doctor, nurse, mortician... Anyone familiar with phlebotomy."

I frowned. "So, a large pool of suspects."

"Maybe. Here's the curious thing about exsanguination — it takes a long time. On my table, gravity does the work. The blood and bodily fluids go through a drain in the table into a sink and into the sewer. However, during the embalming process, an embalmer injects a water-formaldehyde solution into an artery, typically the carotid, and, simultaneously, blood will be pushed through the circulatory system and exit from a drainage vein, again, into the sewer."

"So, what about from a live body?"

"Completely draining the body of all its blood would take a long time, unless you had some means of drawing the blood out. A major laceration in the aorta will quickly drain enough blood to cause death, then the loss of blood slows significantly because of no pressure from the heart."

"So, what you're telling me is, it's impossible?" I said.

"Probably," Hagler answered with hesitation.

"Unless?" I prompted.

"Unless it was a vampire." Hagler grinned or did what passed for it. He grimaced like a pirate's Jolly Roger.

"Not funny, Mel. I'm trying to stop a war between the I-5 Dragon Triad and the tongs."

"The supernatural shouldn't be ruled out." He looked at me, and I could see tears gathering in the corners of his eyes.

"I'll talk to Pamela about you staying at the house. I can't promise anything. It's her place, after all." I left before he could ask me anything else, or, worse, start crying in front of me.

10

Madison Park

The upscale, three-story Victorian house I call home belongs to Pamela Linden. I just live here, where my main duties are to bring home takeout and keep the bed warm. She has servants who do everything else. Pamela is a short — just over five feet — very pretty, dynamic woman with dark hair, dark eyes with malachite-colored flecks in them, a dark complexion, straight nose, long earlobes, and a pianist's hands. I'm a detective, so I notice these things.... Noticed them the first time we met, before we went out for drinks. I noticed also she's a powerhouse, taking charge of our dinner orders. I don't mind her straightforwardness.

She works as a commodities trader. Her office is over the detached garage and is the equivalent of a miniature trading floor. She has several assistants. They monitor all the exchanges around the world. On a good day, she makes a hundred grand before breakfast. She never flaunts her wealth to me, though. During the only discussion we ever had about our income disparity, she shrugged and said, "Money pays the bills. It can't buy a relationship."

After half a dozen shots, Uncle Jack would often say money can buy the *next best thing. He never said what the next best thing was. He simply took a sip of Irish whiskey and winked.*

I stood beside my car in the driveway enjoying a moment of quiet. Willie Fong's murder nagged at me. Psychologists dress murder up with lots of fancy reasons, but it comes down to money, love, revenge, or drugs. Fong's murder hit the revenge button. But in his line of work, the usual MO was a double tap to the back of the head. Bleeding him out was too bizarre and much too personal, like slept-with-Count Dracula's-girlfriend personal.

I scrubbed my face with both hands and looked at the clear, blue sky. In just a few weeks, the fall rains would start, and temps would plummet into the fifties and forties for another ten months, with occasional breaks varying from sixties and sunshine to twenties and snow. I needed to solve this case long before the dark, dreary winter months if I wanted to stop a war between the I-5 Dragon Triad and the Seattle tongs.

You might think I was overplaying this aspect of Fong's murder. But believe me, Willie Fong wasn't just some gangbanger. A legend among the triads and number two in an organization that spanned the entire US West Coast, over the years, he had made a lot of friends as well as enemies. His friends would be out for payback.

I looked up at the large picture windows above the garage facing the driveway. Pamela talked to one of her assistants, Paul Wolfheim. It was after noon, which meant Germany's Eurex Exchange must have closed. Which also meant she had time for lunch.

I walked into the front room. It reminded me of a Gilded Age home filled with curios and tchotchkes, the kind of place one had to shuffle around things in little steps. Pamela hoarded artsy stuff. At least that's what she called it. I called it chichi crap but never out loud. She owned the house, and, to be honest, it was one of those little quirks of her behavior I found endearing. I could see in ten years being driven insane by the pretentious disorder, but I put those thoughts out of my mind for now.

Pamela ordered lunch served on the patio, the one uncluttered spot downstairs. It had a view of Lake Washington that would be a crime to obstruct. We had a couple of hours to kill before she had to get ready for the closing bell of the Chicago Mercantile Exchange. This usually meant a quick meal and a longer, more enjoyable time in the sack. Only, sex was the last thing on my mind right now. Don't get me wrong; I looked forward to these trysts. Pamela was an exceptional lover, but I couldn't shake Cassandra from my thoughts.

Pamela noticed something. "What's wrong, Jack?"

Her full lips, curved in a half smile, reminded me of Marine interrogators I met in Afghanistan.

"It's this case I caught," I temporized.

"It must be something else to take your mind off these," she said, undoing the top two buttons of her blouse.

Did I mention Pamela has the perfect figure? The décolletage beckoned, and Cassandra didn't stand a chance. Yeah, I'm a dog, a creature of instincts, not all of them altruistic or even nice.

I won't bore you with details except to say the next hour in a dark, paneled room on a king-sized bed was as good as it gets, and more than some people have in a lifetime. We held each other afterwards and even slept a little. We might have whiled away more time, but my phone beeped.

"Don't answer, Jack," Pamela said sleepily. She clenched me tighter when I made to reach for the offending noise, and for a few seconds, I gave in and snuggled back. But the beep continued and would just keep repeating until I answered. Such is the life of a cop. Pamela knew it too and let go, pinching my ass when I rolled away. I yelped appreciatively.

I listened for a pair of minutes and hung up.

"You have to go," Pamela said before I could.

I frowned, reluctant to leave a warm bed and an even warmer, beautiful woman, but work called. Besides, thoughts of Cassandra had bubbled up again, spoiling the romantic ambience. I couldn't shake the idea she might be free for me to woo. "Could be a break in the case," I said, wincing at the depths of clichés dialog sinks to in times of pressure.

"Dinner tonight at Henry's Off Broadway? My treat," Pamela said as I shrugged into my clothes.

I leaned over and brushed her forehead with my lips, thought better of it, and gave her a lingering kiss on the mouth.

"What was that for?" she asked, surprised by the ardent affection.

"For making me the luckiest guy on the planet."

Yeah, I'm a dog.

11

Grand Pavilion
Hing Hay Park

*A*t noon any day of the week, Chinatown bustles with people. It's not as crowded as Hong Kong, but it's difficult to walk through, and finding a parking place is all but impossible. It's why I use a beacon flasher on the roof of my car. Also, it makes other drivers clench the steering wheel and stare wide-eyed with terror in the rearview mirror. Deep down, the kid in me aches to get out. The Risperdal keeps him at bay... most days.

The call was from Sheila Cummings, a CSI technician. She said she might have something and to meet her at the Grand Pavilion, so I hurried to Hing Hay Park. I had no trouble parking. In fact, this afternoon, I could have driven a semi down Chinatown's main avenue. News of Willie Fong's killing must have spooked people.

Sheila met me on the steps. Yellow police tape still cordoned off the temple. The park was deserted except for a few bystanders taking pictures. Cummings ignored them and ducked under the tape. Her hand motioned me to follow.

Kneeling over the chalk outline where Fong's body had been found, she asked, "What do you see?"

She was looking down and didn't notice my eyes doing their tardive dyskinesia dance all around the crime scene. It took me a moment to roll with the dislocation. Then, I said, "What am I supposed to see?"

"The floor's tiles are clean. Where's the blood?" she asked.

I recalled what Hagler told me about the body being drained of blood.

"I know what Hagler thinks," she said as if reading my mind. "But Fong was beaten, and still no trace blood. No spatter patterns. Nada."

"Impossible," I said, echoing her thoughts this time. I scratched at the scar on the back of my hand, a constant reminder of the bullet that missed me but left my former partner paralyzed from the waist down.

Sheila looked up at me with a knowing smile.

"So, this isn't the primary crime scene?" I asked, acting more like a novice than a twelve-year veteran of the Seattle police force.

She shook her head. "This *is* the primary scene." Sheila took me to the Japanese garden surrounding the pavilion. One set of footprints crossed the evenly raked sand in deep uneven strides. Willie Fong's. "I've been over every inch of this pavilion and the grounds leading to it. I can find no sign of anyone carrying or dragging a body here. And security cameras show the victim ran into the building alone but never left."

"What else do they show?"

"Nada. The cameras went offline at the time of the murder."

"Switched off?"

She shook her head again. "Just a bright flash. The footage is blank."

"For how long?"

"Three minutes. Then another flash of light, and the camera feed starts up again."

I knew the implication: not enough time to siphon Fong's blood into a container and carry it away. "You have a copy of the footage?"

Sheila showed it to me on her smart phone. We watched the last fifteen seconds of Willie Fong's life before everything turned white. "Jesus, he's running like demons are chasing him," the tech observed.

Just like Hagler said. "The question is, what's chasing him?" I looked out upon the precisely raked rows of sand marred by the jarring impacts of Fong's shoes. "Curiouser and curiouser," I muttered, though this was way out of Alice's wheelhouse. I hated to admit it, but the supernatural angle had gained some traction.

"Send me the footage and check other cameras in the area. Let's see where he started running from," I said.

"Will do." She left to do her thing.

It was after 3:00. Too soon to clock out, not that I ever did on a murder. Might as well head to the precinct.

12

West Precinct

Every precinct has its desk sergeant, the guy up front who runs triage on repeat felons, first time offenders, and general riffraff who arrive willingly or are dragged through the front doors. Our desk jockey is Sergeant Liam McCrory, a pal of mine since grade school, when he didn't let anyone make fun of my Irish-Punjabi ancestry. The son of Irish immigrants from Limerick, McCrory is married to a beautiful Irish lass. I'm godfather to his two kids, a boy and a girl. We closed down a lot of bars coming up through the ranks, until the bullet paralyzed him.

Yeah. That scar. It itches like crazy whenever I see him.

"Woman waiting for you at your desk, Jack," McCrory said. He leaned forward and handed me a card. My eyes darted toward the handles of his wheelchair looming behind him, like they always do. Liam ignored the look and added, "Middle Eastern. Says her name is Zaina Khoury."

"*Zah-eena*... It's Lebanese. What does she want?"

"Claims to have information on the tong murder."

"Triad," I corrected him. Maybe I was overly sensitive, but my gut told me, no way the tongs were involved with Fong's killing. "That would be a relief. So far, all I'm getting is weird questions with no answers."

McCrory laughed. "She should fit right in then. Read what's on the back."

I flipped the card over and groaned. The word psychic had been printed in, lurid red capital letters with green shadow. Last thing I needed was another weirdo thinking they could point me to the murderer.

"We still on for Sunday?" McCrory asked.

Every August, McCrory took his boat out into Puget Sound on the first weekend of the Chinook salmon run.

"Wouldn't miss it."

I ran up the steps to the second floor, where my desk sat by a window with a view of Elliot Bay.

Ms. Khoury sat with knees together facing the stairs. She seemed to know me even before I approached. She cocked her head, studying the way my eyes do their TD thing, giving her the once over like a wolf searching for prey. She didn't blink in surprise, sniff, or do anything, as if she had expected it.

She had dressed conservatively in a dark, ankle-length skirt, gray blouse, and black headscarf. My brain collated her physical traits: narrow face, thin lips, and high cheekbones; dark eyebrows slanted toward the bridge of a thin, angular nose but stopped short of forming a unibrow above dark eyes; no jewelry except for a single, plain, pearl necklace.

She waited patiently for me to speak.

My stomach tightened with the way she followed my path across the room with open curiosity, but I couldn't place what bothered me.

I slid into my chair, taking two quick breaths and two long ones to calm my paranoia, just as Hilde Kersten, my grade school counselor, taught me. Her grandfather had been Himmler's masseuse. "I don't believe in any psychic hocus-pocus," I said as a way of introducing myself. "No offense," I added, meaning it.

I knew a lot about the mystical realm and its magical phenomena through my Punjabi grandparents, who were big believers in the stars guiding human actions. And let's face it, the Irish have their mysteries — leprechauns, pookas, and selkies. Me, I'm a second-generation American, and old-world beliefs don't have any hold on me... so I remind others and myself.

Khoury tilted her head, and beneath the scarf, I could see a few strands of white in the black hair at the temples. The white really didn't tell me anything about her age. She could be thirty or fifty. She said, "It's unorthodox and not usual procedure, I'm sure, but knowledge of crimes is not limited to this plane of existence, detective." Her voice purred melodiously amid the bustle of the squad room. It also murmured with a suppressed current of intrigue, twisting my gut even more, and I had to keep my hands on my desk to keep from scratching my head about her. Her surreptitiousness made me wonder if her connection to the case went beyond so-called psychic phenomena.

I tried to picture her as the murderer, inserting herself into the investigation, but dismissed the idea because of her size. She was hardly big enough to overpower Willie Fong, let alone carry around the heavy equipment necessary to drain his blood.

Before I could tell her to get lost, Khoury stood and smiled down at me. I couldn't help but check out her incisors, thanks to Hagler's vampire reference. They were normal and white like the rest of her teeth.

She said, "I'll be back after the next killing."

I'm the one used to ending interviews, so her abrupt departure took me aback for a moment. "You're very sure of yourself," I said quickly before she could turn away.

"Sadly, yes."

"You know the killer?"

She shook her head. "I know he will strike again, detective."

I rolled with her pronouncement and watched her leave, hips swaying from side to side with a belly dancer's grace, yet not in an overtly sexual manner. All the cops in the room eyed her as she disappeared around the corner down the stairwell. A couple of them looked at me enviously.

She's probably a Sagittarius and can't help the sexual thing, I thought. Astral signs aside, my gut told me something about her didn't add up; and, in case I didn't believe it the first time, it kept asserting, *We've surely got trouble, right here in Emerald City.*

Yeah, I like musicals too.

13

West Precinct Parking Garage

Downtown Seattle is a lot of buildings crammed together. The police garage is below ground, and walking to your car is like trekking through tombs. It drips, and the air is musty. Most people spend just enough time here to get to and from their vehicles.

Me, I sit in my car and think. I go through the day, obsessively, I suppose, rehashing everything I said, making certain I said it correctly. I have this thing, related to my condition treated by the Risperdal, of fitting everything together perfectly. Mama tells the story of how at age three I searched every room in the house and even looked in the refrigerator to find a missing piece to a jigsaw puzzle.

By now, you're wondering how this hoser ever got to be a cop. I think about that myself. On the other hand, I'm damn good at my job. The only unsolved case on my record as a detective so far is the triple ferry homicide.

Quitting time. I sat in my car going over the Chapman family murder case. In a year, nothing had panned out. Nobody saw anything except a stoner ferry hand, who fingered Seattle's mayor as the killer. It ate at me because I knew who it did, but the piece of the puzzle I needed to prove my gut right had eluded me for a year. And now, my suspect, Willie Fong, was stretched out on Hagler's table offering up supernatural clues as to how he died and who killed him. With Seattle's rainy season only a few weeks away, I didn't want to go through another dreary ten months of clouds and gloom with a second unsolved murder on my hands.

I tried to put the case away in its own compartment. In a couple of hours, I was meeting Pamela for dinner at Henry's Off Broadway. It's where we had gone for our first date, and tonight was our one-year anniversary. Otherwise, she wouldn't have suggested it. I had to be present.

My phone had other ideas. The caller ID flashed *CSI tech Cummings*. "Tell me some good news, Sheila."

"Depends on your point of view, Doyle. From my perspective, it's successful. I don't know if it helps your case any, though."

I chopped off the gut-wrenching thought the world was out to derail my career. The unexpected paranoia had me checking the time. Yeah, twenty minutes until a dose of Risperdal. Close enough. I gulped a tablet from the pill bottle I keep with me at all times and noticed I'd have to refill the prescription soon.

"Give it to me straight."

"Willie Fong left the I-5 Dragon's gang headquarters on Jackson Street just minutes before he was murdered. A minute after getting into his car, he started driving erratically. He slammed into a light pole on Maynard on the east side of the park, exited the vehicle, and ran into the Hing Hay pavilion."

"Anyone in the car with him?"

"Street cams don't show anyone. I checked out the car, and he was definitely alone. The car's in the impound lot, if you want to see for yourself."

"Later," I said, thinking of Pamela. "Send me the footage you have."

"Roger that."

"Something else?" I asked. No, I'm not a mind reader or even intuitive. I am an inveterate observer of human behavior. When you have the problems I have, you tend to study the people around you to make certain you're doing things right and no one is getting suspicious you have anything wrong with you. A tightly drawn-in a breath told me she had more to say.

I could hear Cummings self-congratulatory smile as she spoke. "I checked out Willie Fong's place of residence. Did you know he lived in a small bungalow near Green Lake Park?"

I did know and said so.

"Well, here's what I'm betting you don't know. He was a gardener, among many things — one of them very interesting."

I liked Sheila, had worked with her on other cases, and respected her abilities. So, I didn't reply through the annoyance building up inside me like a volcano ready to erupt at her drawing out the *dénouement* of her story. That and the Risperdal cooled my steam. I said, with what passes as affable for me, "What's that?"

"Willie had a special setup in his second bedroom. A shrine, with enough incense burning it's a wonder the house hadn't burned down yet, and, get this, a pentagram drawn on the floor." Sheila paused for the finale. "The guy was a freakin' warlock, like Harry Potter."

During my sheepish silence over not uncovering this tidbit about the deceased myself, I studied the pics of the room she sent me. They showed everything she described as well as a baroque painting of Baphomet, the horned god the Knights Templar worshipped. Below his devil-like depiction floated Hermes, the god of magic, wings fluttering like a hummingbird on steroids.

I thanked her and ended the call but didn't drive away. I stared out the windshield at a drip from the ceiling that plunked hollowly on the hood of my truck with what might have been infuriating monotony to others but was fascination to me. In twenty more minutes of sitting, I counted eighty drips. The regularity soothed me and helped my brain concentrate on Willie Fong's last moments.

Willie must have run to Hing Hay Park because he knew a thing or two about demons and hoped the Grand Pavilion temple would protect him. Unfortunately, while his warlock avocation might have watched over him in the triad culture, it hadn't shielded him from the psycho who siphoned all the blood from his body.

I sighed. *Never bring a bygone mystical rite to a vampire feast.*

Yeah, I was kidding. I wouldn't pursue the vampire angle no matter how much folklore, witchcraft, or psychic bullshit piled on the case.

That left me only one avenue.

14

I-5 Dragon's Headquarters
Chinatown

S eattle's Chinatown is half the size of San Francisco's. Businesses are
 bunched together, nearly on top of one another. You could spit from
the window of the I-5 Dragon's hangout onto the awning of the Good Luck
Noodle House. And don't think it never happens. The undercurrent of
tension between the Dragon Triad and the traditional Seattle tongs is a
river of discontent.

For the most part, the tongs are peaceful benevolent associations created
to protect their members and keep the peace. Sure, they bend the rules, a lot.
So do I, and you do too when it suits you. But for the most part, they're into
gambling and smuggling — goods, not people, guns, or drugs.

The I-5 Dragons, on the other hand, are into all of those bad, illegal
things the tongs won't touch. Especially drugs, because Seattle is a huge
market. Rich suburbanites, wealthy urbanites, and those too dumb to
realize stuffing cocaine up your nose or shooting crystal meth into your
veins is a long slide into emptiness. My uncle sipped his Irish whiskey and
intoned, "Cocaine, meth, and heroin are Darwin's way of culling the stupids
from the herd."

Don't get me wrong here. I'm not giving the Dragons a free pass. They're the worst, if not the most recent, of history's criminal entrepreneurs. It's just that idiots make their brand of criminal depravity possible.

I had an hour to kill before I met Pamela and decided to retrace Willie Fong's last moments on Earth. So, I parked in front of the Good Luck Noodle House, which had me shaking my head. Finding a parking spot on a weekday evening was beyond unusual into the realm of unheard of.

Thanks to Sheila Cummings, I could trace the enforcer's last moments via video. I felt eyes following me as I took up the trail at the I-5 Dragon's doorstep, though no one came outside to ask me what I was doing.

Fong's car had roared west on South King Street. Two blocks later, it smashed into a streetlamp at Maynard Alley South. The impact skewed the steel pole at a severe angle. He had hit straight on as if aiming for it. Why would he do that? It made me think someone must have been with him. But the video showed no one but Fong.

Next, he burst out of the car and ran the half block toward Hing Hay Park, glancing over his shoulder every other step. Hagler had been right. He ran like demons were after him. Even in the grainy picture, I could see he was deathly afraid of something. But the street cams showed no one... nothing chasing him.

I stood outside the entrance to the pavilion, watching a fuzzy white screen on my phone. Fong's last moments were wracked with fear, not at all fitting the man's legendary status among the triads. I had expected him to go down in a hail of bullets *à la Scarface*.

Malvern's question about the ferry terminal murders nagged at me. Fong's death was brutal, as if the killing was personal. The question was who. Everyone had been accounted for: Andrew Chapman was an all but a corpse at the Greenbrier Nursing Home. His cousins squabbled over pulling the plug on the machines keeping him alive and had Willie Fong to thank for their inheritance. Meanwhile, Uncle Lo said the tongs weren't involved. And yeah, I believed him. The suspect pool wasn't shallow; it was non-existent.

The feeling of being watched returned. Someone else had a reason for being here. I know what you're thinking — I spun around and saw the killer standing behind me. If only real life were a cliché. When I turned around, William Chen stood across the street staring at me.

Chen ran the I-5 Dragon Triad. Compared to the tongs, the Dragons were relative newcomers to Seattle, bringing drugs and guns to what had been a peaceful society for the last thirty years. So far, in spite of their presence, they had left Chinatown alone. I had a lot to do with their lack of inroads.

"Captain Billy," I called out. He didn't appreciate the nickname. I didn't give a shit.

He should have waited for me to cross the street. It's a face thing. An old-time leader such as Uncle Lo would have understood. He led the Good Luck Tong with a deft touch, a gentle nudge, and a soft word. Chen was a product of the twenty-first century. Face was an impediment to him. He used a baseball bat and a bullhorn. When those didn't work, people disappeared.

Two of his goons sidled up next to me. The bulges in their waist-bands were compelling. They escorted me the fifty feet across the street. Chen was shorter than me but stockier. Standing on the four-inch curb, he was an inch taller. Maybe the face thing wasn't entirely foreign to him.

He dressed casually in a white suit and open shirt that revealed a pair of dragons on his chest shooting red, yellow-tipped flames above the collar. More dragons circled his wrists, and I knew, from having him strip-searched at the precinct, that on his back Smaug laid waste to Lake-town. Imagine, a fearsome triad leader a big fan of *The Hobbit*. Ink was standard among the I-5 Dragons. The more tats, the higher a person was in the gang. As the leader, Chen was a walking mural.

His eyes narrowed until I doubted he could see anything. "Who killed Willie Fong?" he asked, as if I had been hiding the answer the last day and a half.

"Haven't a clue, Billy." It was the truth, but Chen wasn't having any of it. A car pulled up at that moment. It really did, just like something out of Hammett or Spillane. I noticed we were standing in a blind spot between street corner cams.

"Seriously?" I said. "You're not so stupid, Billy."

Chen reached into his coat pocket and pulled out a roll of bills. I could see they were hundreds. He shoved the wad into my coat pocket. "Find his killer then tell me."

"Or what?" I really was curious. I figured he'd say something trite like, 'I take the money back and something else that's even more valuable to you.' But he surprised me.

He pointed at the man on my right, a gangbanger named Benny Yee. He held a smart phone and had filmed the drop into my pocket. "Or I show everyone you taking money from me, and your career as a cop is over."

He got into the car with the two goons and drove off.

I didn't count the wad. The amount didn't matter. William Chen had trapped me neatly. It was worthy of Uncle Lo.

15

Henry's Off Broadway

Capitol Hill, the scene of a short-lived experiment in anarchy called CHAZ — the Capitol Hill Autonomous Zone. Short-lived is an understatement. It broke down immediately. Humans aren't made to live in a state of disorder without authority. We basically have a social contract mindset. Most of us can't live alone, don't even want to. In the twenty-first century, reliance on others is a given in a country as developed as the United States. Which is why when someone tears the social fabric, even murdering triad criminals, as a society, we expect somebody to do something about it, and by somebody, I mean me, though it would have to wait.

My hour had come and gone. Though Henry's Off Broadway was only a few minutes from Chinatown, I was going to be late. Pamela and I had been together for a year now, and she knew the crazy hours cops kept. Still, she was a stickler for punctuality.

Even with the flashing blue roof light, the drive had its hazards.

My mind kept replaying fantasies of Cassandra and the separation from her husband. I still loved her, which elated me and also made me sad, because Pamela was a great catch. And yet, I drove toward our anniversary like a madman pining over an old flame who had chosen the dowdy King County coroner over a dashing young cop on the fast track upwards.

Pamela deserved better than me.

To add insult to injury, I still hadn't talked with her about Hagler staying with us. He may have gotten the girl, but now he was about to lose her, and as happy as the possibility made me, I couldn't leave the guy hanging.

I pulled into the brightly lit parking lot and parked the car myself. When the valet objected, I flashed my badge and walked inside.

Pamela sat at the table where we first had drinks. I checked my watch — ten minutes after the hour. As soon as I entered, she looked up from the menu at me. Her smile wasn't frosty. So far, so good.

Dinner came and went. The waiter didn't intrude. Not that there was anything to intrude upon. By coffee and crème brûlée time, I hadn't said more than a couple of sentences. I was hashing our special night like a rookie on his first stakeout. She arched her plucked and stenciled eyebrows at me, her way of telling me I'd better fix it quickly.

"I'm sorry, babe," I said into the silence. "It's this case I'm working. No leads, though I'm certain it's somehow connected to the triple murder from a year ago."

"Why do you think so?" she asked.

I shrugged and answered with my best Irish glibness, "My gut."

"Ah, yes, the famous gut," Pamela said. She swirled the wine in her glass and stared at me through its red lens. People really do that, and I was curious what she saw. Instead, I heard, "Going with your gut is inherently uncertain and does not guarantee a good outcome."

I mimed flipping a coin in the air. "Thought you used it with your commodities trading," I said, spooning the last bite of crème brûlée into my mouth instead of offering it to her. Maybe the comment on instincts upset me, but I don't think I would have done the same thing if Cassandra had said it.

Pamela shook her head. "I use a highly sophisticated algorithm based on research as a market predictor. It has a 93.7 percent success rate."

"Well, my gut has a one hundred percent success rate."

She looked at me askance. "You've never been wrong."

"Not when it comes to a case."

Pamela's forehead furrowed, and her eyes narrowed through the red wine prism.

My tardive dyskinesia worked overtime, eyes darting everywhere from the dessertspoon to her cleavage to the waiter halted two steps from our table in midstride like a statue, waiting to see if now was a good time to clear the rest of the dishes. Disapproval descended like pall out of film noir. It might have resolved itself, but the classic interruption happened instead. My phone rang, and I answered.

I listened for a pair of deep breaths then slipped the phone into a coat pocket. "The case just got weirder. I have to go."

"Go," Pamela said, her voice soft, which was worse than brittle coldness. "I'll fool around with the waiter."

We both laughed. You know, the sharp laugh of awkwardness. I wondered if it wouldn't be a good thing; then I could be with Cassandra. I didn't say that, of course. I pecked Pamela on the cheek, which was just as sad.

PART II

COPLAND

16

Greenbrier Nursing Home

The Greenbrier Nursing Home parking lot was empty when Geneva Bowen pulled into her usual spot by the front door. *Good*, she thought, not wanting to run into the ghoulish cousins looking to steal Andrew Chapman's life and money. Once had been enough, though she asked the night- and day-duty nurses to text her if they showed up again. Geneva didn't know what she'd do, but, somehow, she'd stop them from pulling the plug on Chapman.

The automatic doors whooshed open, and Geneva strode toward the reception desk. Murray, the security guard, didn't acknowledge her, his nose buried in a book. The building was unusually quiet even for a nursing home. Clara, the night nurse at the front desk, waved her through with a smile and went back to studying her computer screen. *That's odd*, Geneva thought. Usually, they chatted. She headed down the first-floor corridor, her shoes clicking against the linoleum in the eerie quiet. A cold shiver shot through her shoulders, and, suddenly fearful, she quickened her pace. The door to Chapman's room stood ajar, and she rushed through it.

Her eyes darted first to the monitor. Chapman's pulse beat steadily, his vitals normal. The ventilator pushed air into and out of his lungs with a steady hum. Breath exploded from Geneva's mouth, and she sagged against the doorframe, thankful everything was normal, at least normal for Chapman.

The EEG machine clicked softly in the silence, and its screen continued to show a flat line. Geneva knew better. The strange happenings during her last visit were proof Chapman's life was more than ventilators, EEGs, and monitors... Much more. She wasn't a true believer in the occult, but she didn't discount it either, especially after what she had witnessed yesterday.

The aura bearing Chapman's face rising out of his body and vanishing through the open window into the dark Seattle night hadn't been some ghostly apparition from a dream. It had been as real as herself.

Something had triggered the response. Only moments before, she had been reading from the detective's report about how Willie Fong was most certainly the man responsible for the murder of Chapman's husband and adopted Vietnamese girls.

All the next day at work, she wondered about Fong's death and finally at the end of the exhausting shift had concluded it couldn't possibly have been a coincidence. Somehow, Chapman had exacted retribution for the deaths of his loved ones. Geneva had no proof, just an intuitive sense of rightness developed over thirty-five years of nursing.

Fong's killing filled Geneva with an exhilaration she had never encountered in her work as an ER nurse. A feeling of relief for victims of senseless violence caused by stupid hateful people, by drunk drivers, gang shootings, and abusive parents. A feeling of right-eousness, even, that justice had finally been meted out against the I-5 Dragons for the pointless murder of her niece, Andrea. The vengeance had been building like a furnace continuously stoked for two years — until it blossomed last night, when Chapman's aura climbed out of his inert, frail body and raced into the night to kill Willie Fong.

At last, alongside the pent-up rage burning deep in her heart, a sliver of hope now existed. Hope that the Bible's promised vengeance — an eye for an eye and a tooth for a tooth — would be meted out to those who destroyed the lives of others. And that there could be such a thing as justice for victims. And along with justice and vengeance, at last, for those living with unforgettable and crippling loss, there was the third leg of righteousness' holy trinity — redemption. Geneva wept, for she had found redemption for her weakness in not punishing Andrea's killers herself.

Blood surging through her body, muscles shaking, face flushed, eyes glowing with the zealousness of retribution, she must have looked to anyone peering into the room like an avenging prophet out of the *Old Testament*. Yet, she looked fondly upon the young man lying motionless in front of her. She touched his cheek as a mother would a sick child and vowed to help him achieve peace in this world and the next in any way she could.

Geneva kissed the fingers of her right hand and placed them on Chapman's forehead. She whispered a benediction like anointing the righteous. Then, closing the door so no one could listen in, she settled into the chair beside the bed. From her oversized handbag, she took out the manila folder with the logo of the SPD on it. When her brother had asked about her interest in the I-5 Dragons, Geneva lied and explained many of the gangbangers ended up at Harborview ER, and she wanted to know about them for work.

"Andrew," she said warmly, addressing Chapman by his first name to show she was as devoted to him as he had been to his murdered husband and daughters. "I know you took care of the gangbanger who killed your loved ones. But all of the I-5 Dragons are responsible. It's time we stop every last one of them."

The lights dimmed briefly, and the EEG machine scribbled wildly across its silver screen. Geneva bent her head in a prayer of thanks at the mystical signs showing Chapman not only heard her but also agreed to the unholy bargain to wipe out the I-5 Dragons.

17

305 Ferry Dock

The 305 Ferry Dock wharf is a broad expanse of pavement leading to a pier set on massive wooden pilings driven into Elliot Bay. Yeah, wood. Water's lower oxygen levels mean the pilings can last pretty much indefinitely, and treated lumber can withstand salt and brackish water.

From the wharf, 70,000 drivers and pedestrians a day board ferries from Seattle to Bainbridge Island and other spots along the Olympic Peninsula and back. At night, looking at Seattle from an arriving ship, the city is a mishmash of tall, brightly lit buildings stretching from the shore and up toward Capitol Hill. A neon-lit Ferris wheel on the shore gives the city the appearance of a non-stop carnival, where all kinds of fun and games await disembarking passengers.

No games awaited me this evening, and no fun loomed in my future. An unsmiling Sandra Liu lifted the police tape for me. Twice now in two nights, we met under unappealing circumstances.

"What is it?" I asked.

"Two dead," she answered in a flat voice.

My stomach clenched thinking of the ferry murders from last August. "Civilians?"

She shook her head. "One of them is a member of the I-5 Dragons, and the other a wannabe triad member."

The grim look on her face echoed my thoughts. *Two more dead Dragons. We were skating dangerously toward retaliation and possibly a war.*

"Witnesses?"

Liu pointed to a family shivering beside two uniforms. "Mother, father, and kids returning from a stay with grandparents on Whidbey Island. They were the last off the ferry and had stopped to readjust some gear on the roof when two men in ski masks carjacked their vehicle and took their cell phones. Parents did the smart thing and gave up the car.

"A deckhand exited the building and recorded what happened on his phone. Every light in the parking lot exploded just before a bright, white light engulfed the car. Shots were fired, and it swerved into the barrier. After no movement for a while, he approached the vehicle. The two men were lying on the seats. He called 911."

"Somebody shot them?"

Liu shook her head. "You have to see for yourself. It's Willie Fong all over again."

Darkness surrounded the car, so I decided to speak to the carjack victims first.

They were a young family; the parents and two toddlers could have been on the cover of the PTA's *Our Children Magazine*. They told the same story Sandra Liu did only with frightened squeaks and a lot of choking back fear. When I asked if they saw anything out of the ordinary, the father pointed at the car.

By now, klieg lights lit up the wreck. The car's bumper had caved in, the hood sprung, and the airbags fired. The shooting had taken out the windshield. The two victims had battered faces, but that could have happened in the crash. Otherwise, not a whole lot of damage. Certainly not enough to kill a couple of gangbangers.

Hagler hadn't shown up yet, but I didn't need his expert opinion to see neither of these guys had been shot. No bullet wounds and no blood pools either. Just like Willie Fong, they had been drained of blood as if some over-enthusiastic vampire had sated himself.

According to the deckhand who called 911, the bright light continued for a couple of minutes before stopping. "Like someone threw a freakin' switch," he emphasized several times, waiting for me to write it down in my notepad.

Not enough time, according to Hagler, for machines to remove blood from one body let alone two.

I peered through the passenger window. The ashen corpses lay across the front seat with looks of pure terror contorting their faces. It was way beyond the proverbial seeing ghosts. It was the look of fear on drowning men, clawing at the surface of the water trying to get a breath of air.

I scratched my head, metaphorically and literally. None of this made any sense.

"More vampires, Jack?" Hagler's voice carried across the parking lot like a foghorn on Puget Sound. He wore the same rumpled clothes from this morning, and his face twitched in an expression of the second and third stages of grief — anger and bargaining. He must have talked to Cassandra, and she nixed his pleas to come home.

I said, "Two more triad deaths, Mel."

He stuck his head through the shattered windshield. "Can't say for certain until I get them on the table, but it looks as if the cause of death is the same as Willie Fong — exsanguination."

"So where did all the blood go?"

"Vampires," Hagler repeated. He clicked his tongue against the roof of his mouth. "You talk to your girlfriend about me staying at your place?"

I had completely forgotten about it, my mind being assaulted by a dozen other problems. "You can stay," I said, wondering at the same time how I was going to convince Pamela the husband of my ex was going to crash in her spare bedroom.

"Thanks," Hagler said, relieved.

"Don't mention it," I answered. Our conversation was saved from any more embarrassment by a ruckus at the tape. Sandra Liu was holding someone back. "Catch me when you're done here," I told Hagler and headed toward the patrolwoman.

18

305 Ferry Dock

E instein said, "Coincidence is God's way of remaining anonymous," which raises its own epistemological conundrums. On one hand, a detective is a fool if he considers events in a murder investigation a coincidence. On the other hand, one can stretch a remarkable occurrence of events too thin. Take Shakespeare for example. The Bard was forty-six years old in 1610 when the original translation of the King James Bible came out. Psalm 46 in this version has shake as its forty-sixth word, and the forty-sixth word from the end is spear. Coincidence? Or did Francis Bacon, who helped translate the King James Bible, engineer that relationship to show future scholars he was the actual author of Shakespeare's plays?

Coincidence is the ridiculous and the sublime.

I'm paid to know the difference.

The commotion had a huge "this ain't no coincidence" written all over it. Liu was arguing with a short woman in a black headscarf who seemed overly eager to get to the crime scene — Madam Khoury, the so-called psychic. A grumbling suspicion of trouble vexed me like a pebble in my shoe. Supernatural crap aside, why was she really here?

I plodded toward them. "I know her," I said to Liu. She moved on, but not before muttering in the gutter patois of the Hong Kong underworld, "Looky-loo." At least that's the uncensored version.

"She doesn't like me," Khoury said, nodding her head toward the patrolwoman.

"Can you blame her? You make her job difficult." I didn't lift the police tape.

"You're not going to let me in?" she asked.

"What are you hiding?" I said, deciding the world-weary no-time-for-bullshit approach was best.

She took it in stride. "I sensed what was happening and came down here to offer my help."

I snickered. She didn't frown, and I said, "You have a psychic finger on the pulse of evil in Seattle, and it brought you here?"

"In a sense, you're right," she answered in a soft voice with just the hint of an accent. "The psychic world is connected to Earth's magnetic field. It's how I knew the men were dead."

A police scanner made more sense, and I didn't bother to hide my disbelief. "I'm sure a lot of people died tonight. Why these two?"

She said with asperity as if talking to a child, "I know how they died."

I knew Liu wouldn't tell her anything, and she couldn't see the bodies from her spot behind the tape. "How's that?" I asked with jeer in my tone.

"The blood was drained out of their bodies."

See what I mean about coincidences? And yet, she didn't look the part of a killer of gangbangers. But she could be working with a guy who did. "And you know this how again?"

"The Force."

"Like *Star Wars*," I scoffed.

"I can help," she insisted, not taking the bait. "You're in way over your head, detective."

"Because you helped whoever did this?"

That got under her skin. Her lips curled in a frown. "The person who did this doesn't need any help. He's already too powerful. And if you try to stop him, you'll end up the same as those two men in the car."

I ducked under the tape and grabbed her by the elbow. In Lebanese culture, this is a big deal. No man, not even relatives, can touch an unmarried woman. She didn't say anything. She just eyed my hand as if it belonged to a leper. I let go and pointed to a place away from the klieg lights with a little more privacy. Sandra Liu's eyebrows shot up, and I motioned her to stay with the crowd of reporters gathering behind the tape, who were sure to connect the dots between Willie Fong's killing and those two pug-ugly gang-bangers.

"What aren't you telling me?" I asked Khoury when we were alone.

"I am familiar with the psychic energy surrounding the Earth. I can help you stop the killer."

"Because you know who he is?"

"Of course not. But I can track him. I just need to get close to a crime scene." She gestured toward the ruined Subaru, and I noticed she held her right elbow against her jacket as if cradling something.

My hand went to my Glock. "What are you hiding?"

She rolled her eyes. "You don't need a gun." I kept my hand on my service weapon while she slowly reached into her jacket and brought forth a red case the size of a large smart phone. It had a loop antenna on one end and an upright antenna at the other. A thin black needle on a glowing green dial swung back and forth. With each sweep of the hand, the device emitted soft, distorted wails like a theremin.

"What the hell is that?"

"It's an EMF... An electromagnetic field detector. It measures the radiation that occurs naturally in Earth's magnetic field and is emitted from other sources where direct current is present. In this case, from someone using the Earth's magnetic field to travel on the astral plane."

"Astral projection as a way of killing people," I said incredulously.

She stared back, serious.

I burst out laughing. "Christ, you're a goddamned ghost hunter."

"This has nothing to do with ghosts. The electric field generated by a human can be very strong when directed by a powerful mind. Your killer is using the astral plane to reach his victims and drain them of blood."

I waved her off. "Get out of here. We'll solve this without your fancy ghost busting devices."

She took my dismissal better than I thought but said with earnest, "You will come around, detective. Without me, you will fail."

She walked toward a blue Mercedes, got into the driver's side, and drove away. *Ghost busting pays well*, I thought. I started to turn and saw another car — a tan Volvo — follow her. It didn't act like an obvious tail. But then, there's no such thing as a coincidence at a murder scene. I snapped a picture with my phone. The light over the license plate was out, and the guy driving had a hat pulled down covering the left side of his face. He had a cigarette in his left hand. Probably nothing. On the other hand, I couldn't rule out him being a member of the I-5 Dragons who had concluded, like me, that Khoury was connected to the murders.

Liu tugged at my elbow. "What's her game?"

"Ghost busting," I answered. We both laughed. "What do you need?"

"Hagler wants to see you," she said.

19

---

305 Ferry Dock

Whenever police put up caution tape and klieg lights, gawkers gather like moths to a flame. It's human nature, I suppose. My nature is to look over the crowd for anyone suspicious. There's a lot of money in this town thanks to Microsoft, Amazon, Starbucks, and Boeing. As a result, Seattle has its share of fringe lunatics with a lot of free time on their hands looking for something out of the ordinary to relieve their boredom. Baiting cops is just one of the cures.

Walking toward the crime scene, I scanned the crowd. I didn't see any luminous apparitions peering at me from among the usual gawkers. No one dressed in flowing black capes or with fangs for sucking blood either.

Hagler stood beside a gurney, with two of the traditional, black, zippered body bags piled on top of one another. Two of the ME office's finest technicians, Mack and Mickey Sparrowhawk, picked up the first of the corpses and loaded it into the back of an ambulance. The klieg lights outlined their twin faces — the broad noses, full lips, and high cheekbones of their Salish Indian heritage. They lived on the reservation on the weekend and worked in the city Monday through Friday. They rarely said anything, though they snickered a lot as if pleased to give non-Native Americans a final ride in the bus.

Mack or Mickey — it was hard to tell the twins apart — said something to the other in their native language. They both laughed. I don't speak Salish, but I heard the word Sasquatch.

Great, I thought. *What's next? Werewolves?*

"Anything new... different about this crime scene than the Willie Fong case?" I asked Hagler.

He shook his head. "Exsanguination for certain, though, with no obvious wounds or drain sites, I can't tell you how. It's as if the blood just vanished from their bodies."

The Khoury pebble was back in my shoe. I would have to follow up with her whether I wanted to or not. But not tonight. Tonight, I had to face Pamela with Hagler in tow.

A reprieve from that punishment appeared in the form of Captain Malvern dressed in his uniform and a twizzle of red licorice in his left hand. He grunted at Hagler but never took his eyes from mine. Malvern took a bite of candy. "I-5 Dragons," he said, as if I were responsible for the killings.

I told him what we knew.

"Which is a whole lot of bupkis," Malvern said before I could.

Hagler leaned hard against the ambulance, as if hoping not to be seen. Malvern shifted his gaze to the ME. "What are you still doing here?" He didn't wait for an answer. "Get those perps on the slab and have a report on my desk by morning."

Hagler checked his watch. "It's nearly midnight. I—"

"Then you'd better get started." Malvern was scarier than fiction. Unlike the traditional loud, foul-mouthed, ill-kempt police captains of film noir, he was soft spoken, erudite, and impeccably dressed. Malvern implied no threat, just the certainty if Hagler didn't move in the next ten seconds, he would regret his life choice to become a medical examiner.

Hagler's head bounced up and down like a bobble-head doll. He hurriedly banged his fist on the back of the ambulance. The door opened, and he scrambled inside. The techs must have sensed Malvern's impatience, because the ambulance roared away with lights and sirens before the door closed.

The captain turned back to me only after the ambulance sped out of sight onto Alaskan Way. "Doyle, tell me this isn't some move against the I-5 Dragons leading to a war."

"It doesn't feel as if someone's trying to take over the I-5 Dragons," I said. "It's too personal."

"Some weirdo serial killer after gangbangers?"

"Could be... Maybe. Truth is, I don't know what's happening here, captain."

"Well, you'd better find out. I don't want another Wah Mee massacre on my watch. Not three months from retirement," the soft-spoken voice hissed, and a stiff glare radiated from his eyes.

"Yes, sir," I said quietly without any attitude.

Malvern stalked back to his cruiser. The other cops on the scene snapped to attention as he approached, and one tripped over his own feet, slamming his head into the car's searchlight while eagerly trying to open the door for the captain.

"Pitiful," Malvern said in a stage whisper loud enough for the gawkers to hear. He drove in a large circle around the crime scene, and no one relaxed until the cruiser's taillights disappeared through the 305 Ferry Terminal exit.

I blew out a long sigh and leaned against the vic's car. No one wanted another Wah Mee. February 19, 1983. Kwan Fai "Willie" Mak, Wai-Chiu "Tony" Ng, and Benjamin Ng bound, robbed, and shot fourteen people in the Wah Mee gambling club at the Louisa Hotel in Chinatown. A detective on the job at the time told me the killings had been payback. The fact the cops caught the perps was the only reason a gang war didn't start.

The steady beep of a tow truck backing up shook me out of my thoughts. I stepped away and spent the next ten minutes watching the operator load the vehicle on the flatbed. He'd take it to the SPD's garage, where forensic techs led by Sheila Cummings would go over it for clues that weren't there.

Malvern was right — I had a whole lot of bupkis. I needed to talk to Uncle Lo again. I checked the time. Well after midnight, and he wouldn't see me until breakfast. I headed toward my car and home. At least I didn't have to talk to Pamela about Hagler tonight.

20

Madison Park

The upscale suburb of Madison Park sits between Lake Washington on the east and Seattle's Arboretum on the west. On a clear day, you can see across the lake to Bellevue, home of Microsoft, and glimpse Bill Gates' multimillion-dollar lakeshore estate. To the south, Mount Rainier's glaciered volcanic caldera stretches skyward. If Rainier erupts like it did 500,000 years ago, its ice will melt, and mudflows will take out the entire Puyallup River valley. A hundred thousand people will lose their homes. I-5 will become a giant mud bath. The ash cloud will head toward Seattle, and towns from Eatonville to Tacoma will become modern-day Pompeiis. Madison Park and the private Broadmoor community and golf course, where Pamela's home is, won't be spared. Multimillion-dollar homes will become the most expensive tombs in history, à la the Taj Mahal.

The night guard at Broadmoor's gated entrance knew me and my schedule. He waved me through with a grin. I had brought him a bottle of Pamela's best wine from her cellar at Christmas and another on the Fourth of July. She didn't need to know that.

It was after 1:00, and no lights were on in the house. The office over the garage was lit up. Pamela's assistants were undoubtedly using her algorithm to make millions on the European Climate Exchange, where they traded financial instruments for carbon emissions futures.

I tiptoed upstairs. The bedroom was dark except for a soft glow from the streetlights coming through the lace curtains, outlining Pamela nestled under the covers, snoring softly. I crawled into bed as quietly as I could, not wanting to wake her. She wasn't a shrew. She was kind and caring and loving and deserved a whole lot better than me. Yeah, I'm self-critical, but only when I compare myself to others. As a detective, I always think I'm right. My ego can be hard on partners, which is why I work alone. I also close more cases than any other cop in the squad, or the city.

Maybe you see where I'm going with this aside to the story of triad murders. Pamela was beautiful, smart, sassy, and nice. My mind cluttered with thoughts of our aborted date night at Henry's Off Broadway, Willie Fong, I-5 Dragons, a war, Hagler and Cassandra — and I didn't want to bother her before a busy trading day.

She rolled over and snuggled next to me. She pressed her lips against my ear and whispered, "I've been waiting for hours. Do me quick before my boyfriend gets home." She giggled and nipped my earlobe.

I laughed and drew her on top of me. She kissed my brow, and anxieties about the killings and retaliation and the awkwardness of dinner sloughed away.

After, we held each other close, and she drifted off to sleep. I didn't drift so easily. Images of Cassandra throwing pebbles against the windows of my soul kept me awake, wondering what I was doing. She was a mother of two with two more on the way. I had Pamela and was married to the job with no time for a family.

Pamela let me sleep in. She was thoughtful that way. My phone, on the other hand, didn't have a sentimental chip in its circuits. I heard the familiar Timba ringtone of Pop's and sat bolt upright. My father was eighty-three, invalided by a stroke, and needed care. A county health care worker came in three times a week to look after him. The rest of the time, my mother took care of him. She's sixty-seven — yeah, sixteen years difference. They had married for love. They stayed together for the same reason.

It wasn't like dad to call so early unless it was an emergency. I answered before the third ring.

"Pops. Everything all right?"

"I have to go to the bathroom," he whined.

I cringed to hear my father, who had worked as a lumberjack and taught me how to box, speak in a slurred, reedy voice. "Where's Mama?"

"She's not here."

"I'm on my way. Twenty minutes."

I texted mom. No answer. Now I had two parents to worry about, and I almost put my shoes on the wrong feet.

I texted Pamela, thanking her for letting me sleep in and promising to do something nice for her in return. She sent me an emoji of a smiling cat. I called the precinct and explained my situation to McCrory at the front desk. He told me to take care of my dad, and he'd smooth everything over with Malvern. He sent me a picture of a Bigfoot eating licorice.

The clock in the kitchen read 7:19. No telling how long Pops had been holding it. Plus, "Mama not here" could mean anything, from her going to the store, to her lying dead on the kitchen floor from a heart attack. I texted her again. Still no answer.

I try not to worry about these things, but the heart attack on the floor was winning. I hurried — lights and sirens.

21

Ravenna Park

Growing up half Punjabi Muslim, half Irish Catholic affects your psyche, even if you don't know it at the time. Maybe that's why I'm on Risperdal. At any rate, I think my oldest pal, Liam McCrory, summed up the effect best in junior high school.

We were sitting on bleachers at the soccer field watching three gang-banger wannabes — who had made fun of my hooked nose, dark skin, blue Irish eyes, first name, and religious affiliations — writhe on the ground from the beating we gave them. Liam never let me take shit from anyone about my mixed heritage.

He flicked a cigarette at one of the guys and said, "Jack, what the hell kind of name is Darvesh anyway?"

I told him about my mom's parents. "I'm named for a Punjabi grandfather who worked for a small pharmaceuticals company in Lahore before the Partition in 1947. He lost everything when the company president, a Muslim, denounced him as a Hindu. He and his wife first fled to Mumbai, India, where they were attacked for being Muslim. Then they immigrated to the United States."

McCrory's brow furrowed. "Yeah, but your last name's Doyle, and everyone calls you Jack."

"My dad's side of the family. They came here from Dublin after the Easter Uprising in 1916. The British killed a granduncle drinking in the wrong bar at the wrong time. My middle name comes from him."

McCrory chewed that over for a bit, then in an Irish brogue that wasn't altogether fake, said, "Can you even stand yourself?"

I lie awake some nights wondering the same thing.

I unbuckled my seatbelt and was half out of the car before I turned off the engine. I had a key, but the front door was unlocked. Not a good sign. My parents always kept it secured, afraid of intruders. Heart hammering in my chest, I hurried through the kitchen. Empty. I breathed easier, but did not stop. I rushed up the stairs.

Pops could still use his right arm and leg, and had half hauled himself out of the hospital bed to get to the wheelchair. His pajamas were hung up on the railing, and he dangled over the side, half in, half out. "Don't you dare laugh," he said querulously.

It was hysterical.

I got him to the bathroom in time.

Later, I wheeled his chair in front of a huge picture window in the living room, where he could watch the outside world instead of stare at the ceiling. (I'm leaving out the part where I bathed him, helped him dress in fresh clothes, and made breakfast. He could feed himself and was downright ornery if anyone tried to help. Pops is still a tough son of a gun.)

"Where's your mother?" he asked.

I shrugged. "Don't know."

"Don't you have to be at work? I can take care of myself."

I checked my watch. After 10:00. These things take a while. "I'll stay with you." The county caseworker would look in on him tomorrow.

Pops snorted. "I heard about the second triad killings. You've got work to do." He kept current with the news, especially the obituaries. He wanted to "outlive the other bastards."

"I've got time. Besides, we need to find Mama."

He grimaced. Her absence worried him too. "You going to drive around, look for her?"

"Yes. I'll put the team on it too."

This satisfied him, so I went into the kitchen for privacy. Three months ago, Mama wouldn't have been out of the house when the caretaker wasn't here. I texted her for the tenth time since I got here. Still no answer. I called McCrory, gave him what I knew, and asked him to put out the word discreetly for patrol to keep an eye out for my mom. He didn't need a picture. He knew her from growing up together and had one on his phone from a dinner here three months ago.

The kitchen door opened before I hung up, and mom waltzed in humming *Send in the Clowns* from *A Little Night Music*. In spite of the midmorning hour, she looked ready to party. She wore lipstick, mascara, and rouge. Her hair, normally gray, had been dyed black. She had on heels and an evening dress and clutched a small handbag as if coming home from the theater.

If you're wondering if my tardive dyskinesia was working overtime, spotting all the anomalies in her appearance, it wasn't. My observational instincts kicked in, accumulating information most people rarely notice.

Her eyebrows arched in surprise at seeing me.

"Where have you been?" was on the tip of my tongue. Mama beat me to it.

"Why haven't you stopped by to say hello? I have something for you," she said, as if coming home in an evening dress instead of being there to care for an invalid husband who needed help to get to the bathroom to pee was normal. She opened a cupboard and brought out a cloth bag with naan in it. Mom made the best Indian flat bread in the world. And yes, she had a traditional clay oven in the basement.

I put the bag on the counter. "Where were you this morning,

Mama?" I said. "I've texted you a dozen times, and you never bothered to answer. Pops needed you." I sounded like a scolding son.

She laughed and pinched my cheek. "There's nothing wrong, Darv." She always calls me that. Only one other person does. Everyone else uses my middle name, Jack. "I was out and forgot the time. I'm home now, and everything's fine." She handed the bag to me. "Get out and go to work." She pushed me toward the door.

"But Pops—"

"He's fine. Everything's fine." She shooed me away with a smile and practically slammed the door behind me.

Everything wasn't fine, but Mama was home, and maybe it would be okay. At least with her home, I hoped Pops would be looked after. Still... make up, hairdo, party dress, nice shoes, not to mention her attitude — as if she'd done nothing wrong leaving the house when he needed care — troubled me. It wasn't like her. She had always been there for others. Absence when someone needed help wasn't her thing. Ever. I promised myself I would be back later to check on them.

My phone pinged. Uncle Lo wanted to see me right away, a timely reminder I had three murders to solve so all hell didn't break loose.

22

Good Luck Noodle House

*I*n Chinatown, you'd think with the businesses being so close together, there couldn't be any secrets. But Asians love secrets, and they're great secret keepers, only bringing them into the open when they need something.

Late morning, Chinatown usually bustled with pedestrians dodging pedicabs delivering lunches to businesses throughout the downtown Seattle business district. The bicycle delivery guys slipped through the stop-and-go-traffic faster than cars and parked anywhere. We usually had two or three bike-pedestrian run-ins a week. Nothing a stiff middle finger and slew of Cantonese obscenities couldn't handle.

Nada today. The district looked like Seattle during the Covid-19 shutdown. I found a parking space in front of the Good Luck Noodle House and walked into a mostly empty restaurant.

Uncle Lo sat at his usual spot, a pot of jasmine tea steaming on the chipped Formica tabletop. He clapped his hands, and several trays of dim sum appeared, with two or three pieces on each plate. I hadn't eaten breakfast, and the spicy aromas made my head swim.

Still, I waited for Lo to serve — important to let him make the first move. His fingers shook, and a pork dumpling slipped from his chopsticks into a black bean dipping sauce. Dark droplets fluttered across the tabletop. The air grew still. He left it there and chose another, this time deftly placing it on my plate.

We ate in silence. Even the waiters and kitchen help padded silently around the restaurant. At last, laying his chopsticks across a small, chipped bowl with generic Chinese patterns around the rim, Lo leaned back against the booth's ruby red cushions and frowned. "Two more killings. It isn't good for business," he said, gesturing at the mostly empty restaurant.

"It's bad for all the tongs," I agreed.

Lo's eyes narrowed. "Even the Police Tong. If they can't solve these killings, it will turn very bad for them."

Sweat chilled my shoulders. Police Tong didn't refer to the SPD in general but to a secret brotherhood within the department. The brotherhood supposedly had started a few years after the Wah Mee massacre and controlled the gambling and prostitution throughout Chinatown. Plus, the Police Tong kept the drugs out of the district and made it safe for tourists. The brass had never found any proof, but that didn't stop them from continuing the search.

I didn't want to spar with him. I was worried about my parents, my relationship with Pamela, and how I was going to tell her about Hagler and Cassandra. Plus, I'd forgotten to take my Risperdal this morning. I reached into a coat pocket, retrieved the pill bottle, and popped the cap. Three left. Time to renew the prescription. I washed a tab down with jasmine tea and waited several seconds before answering.

"I'm doing all I can, Uncle Lo," I said.

"You must try harder," he insisted, "before the killings cause immeasurable hardship among the Asian community, the tongs, and all of Seattle."

What could I say to reassure him? I had no leads. These killings weren't hits. I didn't care how clever the tongs were; they wouldn't drain blood from their victims. It wasn't how they operated. Plus, the gang unit had heard no chatter of a smaller crew going for the big leagues. I was left with a dubious person of interest — a Lebanese woman inordinately curious about the killings through her psychic, astral-plane, Earth's magnetic field hocus-pocus. In all truthfulness, the murders could have been deemed a public service, if not for the seriousness of the I-5 Dragons hitting back and sending all of Seattle into a shit storm of killings.

"No leads," I repeated aloud for Lo's benefit.

His eyes slitted further. "You met with William Chen."

"Uh-huh."

"He gave you ten thousand dollars. Why?"

Jesus, I thought, trying to ignore the growing bullseye on my back. *How did the old man know?* Even I hadn't known the amount until I looked at the wad in the privacy of my home. One hundred crisp hundred-dollar bills. The kind the bank gave out after the Federal Reserve shipped them to the banks.

"You tell me," I said. "You're the man with the information."

"Maybe he wants you to look the other way when they retaliate against the rivals killing them."

"Unlikely. He's worried like you. Wants the killings solved right away."

"Or?"

"Or he gets his money back."

"You going to help him?"

The question hung in the air between us. Nuances of loyalty to Lo and the police created such a din in my brain, I couldn't sort anything. Suddenly tired of matching wits with a master go player, I got up to leave.

"Where you going?" Lo asked.

"I have three murders to solve. Nothing more I can learn here."

To my surprise, Lo laughed and poured more tea. "Sit. I have good news."

I sat down again.

"The murders aren't hits but revenge," he said.

I had to agree it sure looked that way. The question was who. The best suspect with a motive for revenge against the I-5 Dragons was on life support at Greenbrier Nursing Home.

Lo answered my unspoken question. "Auntie Toy knows what's going on. You should see her."

The first time he suggested I see Auntie Toy had been bothersome. A second time was akin to giving an order. Only, Uncle Lo never gave orders. He always couched them as recommendations. I had no idea what the old man was hiding or the depth of the game he was playing. To refuse to see her could only lead to problems, and likely catastrophe. His not-so-subtle hint about outing the Police Tong was the most formidable of the catastrophes possible.

"I will see her," I said. "Thanks for the tea and the dim sum."

A young man in a suit and tie emerged from the kitchen. He kept his gaze averted from mine and whispered something in Lo's ear.

Lo answered in a dialect I didn't understand. He turned to me and said solemnly, "You have seventy-two hours, Jack."

23

West Precinct

If you think Uncle Lo's prodding is ominous, you should have been in my shoes. A three-day deadline as good as ordered me to solve the case soon, and I'd better take Auntie Toy seriously. Luckily, I have a precinct where I can take a moment to regroup and think.

Some say a cop's precinct is his second home. "A place of refuge from the world outside," Captain Wes Malvern tells every rookie.

Others say the precinct is an officer's real home, a castle where fellow cops will protect him from any evil that stalks his life.

The captain's illusory protection was pierced the moment I walked into the West Precinct's modern, $20-million building. When Sergeant McCrory warned me Khoury was again waiting for me at my desk, I knew there was no way the baggage of my life would be left at the front door.

"How did you let her get by you?" I asked.

He answered, with his broad Irish smile, "You going to close this case by Saturday? Supposed to be a record run of Chinook this year."

Honestly, I didn't think I could close this case if I had a month of Fridays before this weekend, but I gave him a thumbs up and climbed the stair two steps at a time.

Khoury sat at my desk, facing the huge windows overlooking Elliot Bay. A stiff wind kicked up a high chop. A sailboat sliced through it, heading north into the deeper, calmer waters of Puget Sound. I wished I were on it away from all the bullshit of murders and family problems. But only for a second. Then I was back in the precinct and down to business.

Not bothering to say hello, I started right in. "Who was the guy in the tan Volvo following you home last night?"

Khoury's eyebrows arched in surprise, which surprised me. I had concluded from the way the guy nonchalantly followed her Mercedes that they knew each other. She shook her head. I pulled out my phone and showed her the pic I snapped. If she knew the guy, she hid it well, except for a small tic above her left eye. Still, I had nothing concrete to go on, just a hunch she was involved with him somehow.

"You can go," I said, dismissing her with a wave.

She hesitated and looked about to warn me again that I needed her help but decided against it.

"Wait," I said. I showed her the pic again. "Who is this guy, Ms. Khoury? It is Ms., right?"

"Doctor, actually." She glanced at the picture. "I'm sorry. I don't know him. Do you think he's connected to the case?"

"Do you?" I asked.

She bit her lip. "No. He's not your killer."

"You're very sure of yourself, Dr. Khoury."

"Call me Zaina."

"I'll consider it, Dr. Khoury. What's your specialty?"

"I'm not a medical doctor." She rose and held out her hand. I went to shake it, and she handed me a card. "Call me when you wish to discuss finding the real killer."

She left, and I pulled out the top desk drawer to put her card with the other one. It was different than the one McCrory handed me two days ago. The word psychic had been printed on it in lurid red letters with green shadow. No mention of being a doctor. I looked at the new card in my hand. It read *Zaina Khoury, PhD Physics*. It had a phone number and email but no home address. I had the feeling of egg on my face, as if I'd misjudged her. At the same time, my gut clamored at me — Why in hell was a PhD in physics interested in murders? And who the hell was the guy following her?

Malvern stopped beside my desk. "You're going nowhere fast with this case, Doyle," he stated in his way of presenting clichés as if they were enshrined on tablets like the ones Moses carried down from Sinai.

"I've got leads," I insisted, though they were nothing more than phantom descriptions from terrified witnesses. I pointed after Khoury. "She's my chief suspect."

"Her," Malvern scoffed, a red licorice vine hanging from his mouth. "She's barely five feet tall and weighs ninety pounds soaking wet. Does she look as if she could scare anyone to death, let alone siphon their blood?"

True and truer. Khoury could hardly scare a crow out of a cornfield let alone frighten a triad lieutenant. And no way could she handle the equipment to drain a body of its blood. I already knew this. But I didn't believe in her astral travel hocus-pocus on the murders and told him so.

Malvern pulled another long vine of red licorice from his pocket and started chewing heartily, the first one having already disappeared. He ate the candy like a chain smoker used cigarettes. "You've got bupkis. Pull off the blinders. Maybe you could use a little hocus-pocus to get in gear."

"You believe in this astral plane crap?" I asked, at the same time wondering if he knew the true meaning of bupkis derived from the Yiddish *bobke* — goat turd.

Licorice twirled between his fingers like a magician's coin. It was impressive actually, considering how large his fingers were, much more so than what he said next. "My wife goes to a tarot reader weekly. She swears by the readings, says it's why we're still married after thirty-seven years."

I scratched my chin, hoping for some kind of inspiration to get me out of this conversation before I said something stupid. The phone rang, and it was Cassandra. "I have to take this," I said.

"Talk to this Khoury woman," Malvern said.

"Is that an order?"

"It's a suggestion you'd better follow up on, Jack... today, or I'll make certain you don't set foot on McCrory's boat this weekend."

First Uncle Lo, then Khoury, and now Malvern. What was it with these people and paranormal crap? I kept that comment to myself, of course. "Copy that, boss."

I stared at the broad back of his dress uniform as he walked to his office. As soon as the door closed, someone started a slow clap. Snickering followed. I get a lot of that.

Follow-up would have to wait until after lunch. Cassandra agreed to meet me at Chubb's in Chinatown.

24

Chinatown

Chubb's is the only non-Asian restaurant in Chinatown. It also has the best Mexican food in the state. It has a sign on the door in Spanish: Esta comida no es para gringos — *This food is not for gringos. If you can't read the sign, you aren't allowed in the diner.*

The décor does not remotely match the food's remarkable reputation. Inside, it's dingy with a couple of tables that look like they'd been used on the set of a Hollywood bar fight, an ancient non-working pinball machine, and a rusted condom dispenser. People take their food and go. Some sit outside at white plastic picnic tables. No one eats inside.

A single window is where people order food. On the other side sits the largest Mexican I've ever seen. He's a living Pancho Villa, sans pistols and bandoliers, with long mustachios and a three-day-old beard. "Order!" he rasps in a tone that threatens that you'd better know what's on the menu — a faded sheet of white paper pinned to the wall beside the window.

Behind him is a short hall leading to a wide-open kitchen, where three or four cooks are always busy, and not one word of English is ever spoken. A little old lady holding a well-used straw broom sweeps the hall floor in quiet swipes. Everyone smiles at her. She smiles back but never says anything.

Once, when ordering lunch, a fight broke out among the cooks. Knives flashed. The big guy slid off his stool and lumbered menacingly down the hall. I thought I'd have to arrest somebody. Then, the little old lady yelled something in Spanish and brandished her broom at the kitchen crew. They hushed instantly and went back to work. The big guy was trembling.

"You just never know" should be part of every cop's lexicon.

Half a dozen people were standing inside Chubb's waiting for their food when I arrived. Cassandra walked in a couple of minutes later like she owned the place. That's how she looked no matter where she went. At five-eight, 125 pounds of hard muscle, and with cropped blond hair, she had the look of an elite athlete. She had been an alternate on the US rowing team for the Beijing Olympics.

"Cass," I said and gave her a quick hug.

"Darv," she answered. She's the other one who calls me by my nickname. Looking around the place, she smiled. "You remembered."

Chubb's was our first date. I had been a rookie detective assigned to the West Precinct, and Chinatown was my beat. I'm fluent in Punjabi, Pashto, Mandarin, Cantonese, and Arabic. I even speak some Vietnamese and know most of the obscenities in Malay. But no Spanish. So of course I took her here.

We ordered, saying nothing while we waited. Our food came, and once outside, we sat at a small, rickety table at the far end of the eating area.

Cassandra dug into her burrito deluxe as if she were still training for pairs rowing. Hagler had said she was pregnant with twins, though it didn't show yet.

I left my enchilada untouched. It was awkward seeing her, not knowing what she wanted to talk about.

She noticed and said, "I'm getting an abortion and a divorce from Mel, in that order."

She talked the way she ate, decisively. She never left room for debate when she had made up her mind. It's what I loved about her.

(Still love about her. I hate the endless second-guessing people do about their decisions.)

"Why tell me?" I thought I knew the answer and was flattered, though a bit upset about it. Not that Mel and I are friends, but it felt like stabbing him in the back.

"I need someone to go to the clinic with me. Mel won't do it."

Bingo. I put a forkful of corn tortilla, beef, and cheese into my mouth to give me time to think. Not about whether I'd go. I knew I was going. I wanted to answer in a way that didn't make me appear happy about her circumstances and the possibility of being available again.

"Tell me when and where. I'll be there," I said, keeping my voice bland as though abortion to an Irish Catholic, Punjabi Muslim was an everyday occurrence.

She didn't ask, "Are you sure?" I'd said I'd go, and she considered the matter closed. She spoke, thought, and acted in sure, steady ways. She never used three words when one would do. But damn I missed her.

I returned to my food. She eyed me for a few breaths. My eyes darted all over the open space. "Still on the Risperdal," she said. Not a question.

I patted my coat pocket. Cassandra knew my secret. She'd been through the nightmares of my bizarre, repetitive, and at times paranoid behavior when I decided to go off the medication; she stayed with me until normal again, then left when I got down on one knee and opened the diamond ring's velvet box. I never asked why; she never offered an explanation.

"How's the case going?"

"Cases," I corrected, holding up three fingers. "No leads except for a psychic who says she knows who the killer is and how to stop him."

"Talk to her," Cassandra said.

"Uncle Lo and Malvern told me the same thing."

"Listen to them," she insisted.

My eyes narrowed. My TD was under control. My detective instincts, on the other hand, kicked in. "You're fired up about this."

"Psychics know their stuff."

"And you know this how?"

"It's why I didn't marry you, Darv."

I almost spit my food out. "A psychic told you not to?"

She nodded.

Anger roiled inside me. I had to knock it down before I said or did something really stupid. "Bet you're sorry now," I teased. I only managed to control half of it.

"Not at all. The psychic said you'd die if I married you."

The look of sadness in her eyes took the anger right out of my sails. "We didn't have to get married. We could have lived together," I answered, trying to make a joke out the pain riveting my heart to my spine.

She shook her head in a way that always made me want to push errant strands of blond hair behind her ears. Her hair had been long when we dated. "Not if we had children. They couldn't have been christened in the Church."

Right. Cassandra was Irish Roman Catholic through and through. For all her independence and unyielding determination, back then, she never would have gone against Church doctrine or her parents' wishes. Now, I wasn't so certain. After all, she was getting an abortion.

"How are your parents?" I asked.

"Expats in Ireland living the dream. How are yours?"

"Pops is bedridden with a stroke, but still ornery as hell. Mama..." I hesitated, not certain I should tell her what worried me.

Cassandra did this thing she'd always done when she wanted me to speak, and I clammed up; she put her hand on mine.

"I don't know what's going on with her," I confessed. "Dad needed her this morning, and she wasn't home. In fact, it looked as if she hadn't been home all night. She's never done anything like that before."

"Sounds dicey. Could she be ill?"

Mom had never been sick a day in her life. But maybe. "Getting her to the doctor is the problem," I said. "She calls them a waste of money."

"Send the doctor to her." Cass shrugged as if the answer was obvious. She checked her watch. "I have to fly. I'll text you the place and time. Thanks, Darv." She brushed her lips against my cheek and was gone.

She'd eaten the entire deluxe burrito down to the last shred of lettuce. I had worked halfway through my enchilada. I tossed the rest of it, no longer hungry. Too many things on my plate —parents, killings, Chen, Uncle Lo, Khoury, and now an abortion.

I squeezed the bottle of Risperdal in my coat pocket. If life kept up this pace, I'd need to double my dose.

25

Harborview Medical Center

I *love hospitals. When I was growing up, my parents wanted me to become a doctor. My uncle was an attendant in surgery at Swedish Hospital, and, once a month, he took me on weekend rounds to see his patients. Later, while he spent fifteen minutes doing paperwork in the doctor's lounge, I raced wheelchairs up and down the corridors.*

After, he would take me to Victoria's Bakery, where he bought schnecken, crullers, donut holes, and éclairs for his family before taking me home. He let me eat as much as I wanted, which, to my Risperdal-soothed brain, was like dying and going to heaven. At home, Mama refused to let me eat sugar, said it exacerbated my condition. As a seven-year-old kid, I thought exacerbated was some kind of sex problem. Still, I didn't hesitate, and on Sunday mornings, I wolfed down a couple of éclairs, a large schnecken, and four donut holes on the drive home from the bakery. For the next twenty-four hours, I worried obsessively that my penis would fall off. It never did, yet I still check myself the day after eating anything sweet, like crème brûlée.

· · ·

I waited on the first floor, where Harborview's ER was, for Hagler to finish his paperwork in the ME's office on the next floor. The room was quiet — no orderlies hurriedly cleaning gurneys for the next accident victim, doctors yelling "stat," or nurses rushing into cubicles with armfuls of gauze and suture kits. More wheelchairs were lined up near the trauma center entrance than patients waiting in hard plastic blue chairs.

My afternoon had been a bust. No leads. Nothing. And a whole lot of thinking about my ex. I had called Pamela and told her Hagler's story and his request. She said yes with only a bit of frost. When we first met, I had explained what happened with Cassandra. (I left out the year of gambling and drinking.) She replied that the past was the past, and we were the now. *Some now*, I thought, and my eyes strayed nostalgically to the wheelchairs.

While waiting, I decided to follow up on Malvern's order concerning Khoury, sort of. Okay, not really. After a moment of doubting reality, I realized that by accepting the astral plane angle, I might as well be investigating the Tooth Fairy, Easter Bunny, or Santa Claus as the killer.

Instead, standing in the ER, I decided to follow a million-to-one hunch that emerged in my head without warning like the *Hindenburg* zeppelin exploding: What if Andrew Chapman was using his coma as a ruse in order to operate a one-way blood bank with the I-5 Dragons as the donors? Say he had built a vampire-like device capable of draining blood quickly and mimicked Count Dracula to throw everyone off the trail. After all, Chapman, by every account I read, had been a brilliant scientist, reportedly on the short list to win a Nobel Prize. Faking brain death to mete out justice for his murdered family made more sense than Khoury's astral plane mythology or Auntie Toy's vengeful ghost theory.

Like I said, a tenuous idea, but the million-to-one odds were better than the Easter Bunny, though I would have put my money on the Tooth Fairy.

When the Chapman theory occurred to me — more like slammed into my thinking, knocking out all other avenues of inquiry

— something in my brain's peculiar relationship between synapses and neurotransmitters compelled me, beyond what the Risperdal could quash, to follow through with it. My tardive dyskinesia disappeared, my vision narrowed, and I focused with a laser-like intensity that would have been the envy of Ritalin users.

The first person I saw was a nurse behind the ER reception desk. She was Black, tall, and beautiful, with short, curly blond hair and a small mole beside her left nostril. A wide smile invited me to tell her my personal story. (I would never do that to anyone.) Her nametag read Geneva Bowen. Unbelievably, I had a ninth-grade English teacher with the same name. More than once, she sent me into the hall for talking back. Maybe she guessed my secret.

I caught Nurse Geneva's eye, and she came over. "May I help you?" she asked in a voice as inviting as the smile.

I showed her my badge. "I'm working an old case from last year, a triple homicide."

Her face grew somber. "The Chapman family. A terrible thing... Husband and two girls murdered, and him in a coma still." She dabbed a tissue at her eyes. "Sorry. I was on duty the night they brought him in."

"A tragic loss," I said.

"Everyone those triads send here is a loss, detective," she said with such fierce intensity, I wondered who the Dragons had sent here who she was close to.

"The coma... How bad is it?"

"Doctors say he'll never wake up."

I noticed the defiance in her tone. "But you don't agree."

"No sir, I don't. I know he's in there somewhere."

"Any chance he's faking it?"

She shot me a look of pure hatred that vanished with an apology. "I'm sorry, detective. No way he could have been involved in those Chinatown killings."

I hadn't asked, but she volunteered the information as if trying to put me off the scent.

Her smile returned with no warmth in it, which had me

wondering what was going on with Chapman and the nurse. Geneva Bowen had the knowledge to drain a human body of blood. And if her fierce tone was any indication, maybe *she* was my one-in-a-million-hunch killer of Willie Fong and the others, and not Chapman.

And like that, Fong's fearsome reputation as the biggest badass among badasses asserted itself. No way Nurse Bowen or Andrew Chapman could have overpowered him let alone sent him running for his life to the Hing Hay pavilion. My hunch fell apart like a QAnon conspiracy.

Coming down from that high intensity, laser focus left me empty, and I reached out for anything to steady me. Shit, I wondered if this psychic, astral plane crap had something to it after all.

"Doyle!" Hagler's rumbling voice roared through the ER, thankfully ripping away my nanosecond flirtation with the occult.

I smiled apologetically at Geneva. "I have to go. Nice talking with you."

Her faux smile disappeared, replaced by a passionate tone that had all but the pointing finger of *j'accuse* with it. "You're Doyle.... You're the detective on Chapman's case."

"I am," I said, working hard to remain un-flummoxed under her accusatory glare.

She sniffed. "They should pin a medal on the person doing your job for you... bringing those animals to justice."

I didn't agree with her. Not because of the vigilante nature of the killer. Hell, those bastards deserved what they got. I objected because it was my case, my mystery, my jigsaw puzzle, and I wanted... I needed to solve it. And whoever was killing off I-5 Dragons was losing jigsaw pieces, making it impossible for me to solve the puzzle.

I didn't say any of that. I smiled at Nurse Geneva. "If you find out who's killing off the Dragons, let me know, and I'll pin the medal on him myself."

She sniffed and went back to paper shuffling or suture counting, or whatever she did to end conversations with people she didn't want to talk to.

. . .

Hagler piled into the car wearing the same creased suit as yesterday. He smelled of formaldehyde and alcohol.

"You'll have to wash up before dinner," I said.

"Cassie can't get used to the smell either." Tears hung in the corners of his eyes, and exhaustion drew his features downward in a saturnine frown. He glanced at me sideways. "She said she talked to you today."

I didn't want to talk about her, so I changed the subject. "Would a nurse know how to drain blood out of a body?"

"I suppose," he said and added in the next breath, "What did she want?"

"She just wanted to talk." I paused. "Are comas permanent?"

He shrugged. "If the patient has significant brain damage or is in a persistent vegetative state. What did she want to talk about?"

"You. The separation. She still loves you, you know." Yeah, maybe she didn't want to be with him right now, but that didn't mean she didn't love him anymore. "How can you tell about a coma patient? How do you know if he's brain dead?"

"Doctors use several tests. If the patient fails to respond to stimulation... if heartbeat and breathing can only be maintained with a ventilator. A means to know for certain is an EEG. If the patient flat lines, it's a good indication he's brain dead." Hagler furled his lower lip in his teeth and pushed his glasses up his nose a couple of times. "Did she talk about the abortion?"

"No," I lied. "You two need to figure it out on your own." I didn't know how to ask this next thing without sounding as if I'd gone off the deep end, so I just put it out there. "Do you think there's anything to this psychic crap?"

"You mean supernatural phenomena and the like?"

The question seemed to pull him together. At least he hadn't asked another question about Cassandra. I told him about the Khoury woman and her belief the killer had used the astral plane to kill his victims and drain their blood.

Hagler laughed. "It's as good a theory as anything you've got so far. Though I prefer vampires. The Sparrowhawk twins think it's the work of Bigfoot."

The conversation degenerated into flying monkeys and woo-woo shit, which worked for me.

I parked in the driveway. The front door light was off. Not a good sign. My phone rang, and I answered. The soft voice of Uncle Lo said, "Good evening, Jack. I am hoping we can have a word."

Lo must have been very put out to come directly to the point instead of talking about inconsequential matters for a couple of minutes before broaching the subject of an ask.

But I was angry too. Lo had brought up the Police Tong and had wielded the knowledge like a club the last time we spoke. I wasn't inclined to be generous. Besides, the last thing I wanted to talk about tonight was psychic bullshit from soothsayers... even Auntie Toy.

"You gave me seventy-two hours," I answered politely.

"Ah, Jack, I'm afraid we must talk and very soon," the soft voice insisted.

"Not now," I said, much less polite than before.

Silence on the other end. I resisted saying, "Hello, you still there?" Finally: "Tomorrow morning, early."

The phone went dead before I could say yes or no. Lo was pissed. He had let me get away with brushing him off tonight, but I had better be at the Good Luck Noodle House tomorrow or certain SPD brass would get an earful about the legendary Police Tong.

"Who was that, Jack?" Hagler asked as soon as I put the phone in my suit jacket pocket. Another thing about the chief ME: He knew no social boundaries. I had told Pamela earlier he couldn't use the spare bedroom upstairs. He had to sleep downstairs in the den where he wouldn't wander into our room in the middle of night crying about Cassandra. She agreed.

"The guy who does my shirts," I answered with some asperity.

"Yeah, right," Hagler said in a tone that indicated he thought maybe I was banging a woman on the side. Maybe he wondered if it was Cassandra. For the record, I don't cheat on girlfriends. More likely, he knew I had been lying when I said we didn't talk about the abortion. Hagler can be a putz, but he's also smart... like Neil de Grasse Tyson smart. Still, his insinuation that I sleep around did more to piss me off than Uncle Lo's threat at outing the Police Tong. I had to let him know he could only push me so far.

"If you're not careful, Mel, I'll drop you outside the gates, and you can find your own way to a motel."

He let the matter drop.

PART III

WORLDS COLLIDE

26

Greenbrier Nursing Home

Geneva Bowen plodded wearily through the entrance to Greenbrier Nursing Home. The Harborview Medical Center ER had been slammed again as her shift ended, when a bus full of seniors taking a tour of Pike Street Market overturned after the driver fell asleep at the wheel. No deaths, but a lot of serious injuries. She had pitched in as a matter of course. But it had meant arriving at the nursing home after midnight.

She said hello to Murray. The young security officer, reading another book, feet propped up on the desk, grinned and waved her forward.

The late-night duty nurse was a young Chinese-American woman she hadn't met before, so she stopped to introduce herself. "Hi, I'm Geneva Bowen. I'm here to visit Andrew Chapman."

The nurse hastily checked a note on a clipboard beside her computer. "Yes, of course. Clara told me about you... said you're here every night. The Good Samaritan who checks on Mr. Chapman in room 124 every night." The words came out in a rush, and she blushed. "Sorry, but you're kind of famous around here, and when midnight came and passed, I was afraid I wouldn't get a chance to meet you. I—" She frowned. "I'm doing it again, talking too much."

"It's all right," Geneva said with a smile. "It's nice to meet someone cheerful at this hour. You are...?"

"Myrna Toy. I'm new here."

"Are you related to Auntie Toy?"

"She's my aunt... my great aunt on my mother's side. We..." She blushed again. "I'm sorry."

"Really, it's not a problem. Your aunt read my fortune, once... before you were born. It's why I became a nurse."

"Auntie Toy told me my life would be happy if I helped people. It's why I'm here." She bit her lower lip. "These poor souls... I want to help them any way I can."

"I know what you mean," Geneva said. "Has anyone been to see Mr. Chapman?"

Myrna shook her head. "He looks so peaceful, like he's sleeping and is going to wake up at any moment."

If you only knew.

Myrna's eyes teared.

"What's wrong?" Geneva asked.

"It's just terrible what his family is trying to do. I hope the judge never orders him off life support."

Geneva patted Myrna's arm. "Amen."

She strode down the hall, feeling better that at least one person on the staff had Andrew Chapman's welfare in mind.

Geneva tiptoed through the open door. The air smelled exquisitely of the roses and angel trumpets placed around the room in earthenware pots. The ventilator hummed quietly, and the monitor showed his vitals were strong. She bowed her head and uttered a little prayer for the staff taking care of him.

Standing beside the bed, she caressed his cheek and whispered, "Hello, Andrew. It's Geneva." The white line on the EEG machine's screen twitched upward. Nursing home doctors wrote off these fluctuations as anomalies indicative of nothing. Geneva knew better.

"I have more reading for you tonight," she said, pulling the police file from her purse. Before she settled into the chair, she checked the feeding tube and the saline drip. Both had been replaced recently. The skin where the IV had been inserted felt firm and supple, unusual for a long-term coma patient, where the epidermis usually developed an appearance of tissue paper called crepey skin. For her, this was just more proof Andrew Chapman was not brain dead. Indeed, his mind had transcended the limits of medicine and maintained his body far beyond what would be expected.

"You're doing good for the community, Andrew. The gangbangers from the I-5 Dragons executed last night will never hurt anyone again. We still have more work to do. It's time we cut off the head of the snake."

Andrew's eyelids fluttered, and she sensed he was as eager as she to seek revenge for his family's murders.

Geneva opened the manila folder. At the top was printed the name William Chen. She scowled. According to her brother, he had ordered the drive-by shooting where her niece had been killed. No one could prove it though. *That doesn't matter anymore*, she thought.

"Chen's the evil one. He calls the shots," she declared, her voice carrying all the hate and sadness she could muster.

The EEG machine scrawled huge arcs across its tinted green screen.

Slowly, she told him the I-5 Dragon leader's known hangouts.

The room's lights dimmed, their glow replaced by the blazing aura of Andrew Chapman as it rose out of his emaciated body until it stood, straddling the corpse-like figure that seemed to have shrunk even more. Bright blue eyes glared with fury, and thin lips parted in a silent scream of rage. Geneva marveled at how, over the past three nights, his astral body had manifested more definition until it appeared as strong and vibrant as when his family had been alive.

"Godspeed," she whispered. The pulsing apparition vanished through the open window into Seattle's dark night. She rested her chin against her chest and prayed for the swift delivery of justice.

· · ·

At the night duty desk, Myrna Toy looked up from her computer and cocked her head at the crackling hum filling reception. Murray looked up from his reading, mouthing, "What the fuck?"

Starting with Mr. Chapman's room at the end of the hall, the lights flickered in a cascade from room to room as if a surge had blown the wiring. The hall lights dimmed, and her computer screen flickered to static before the image returned.

Myrna quickly went through the security camera footage from each room. The system had gone online just this afternoon, giving the duty nurses a chance to look in on residents and quickly call for help if something appeared wrong. She checked Chapman first. Geneva Bowen sat motionless, head bowed, as if praying. Mr. Chapman slept — or what passed for sleeping in a coma patient. The EEG monitor flickered, and she gasped at the furious scrawls, as if the man's brain were fully functional.

Quickly, she scanned the other rooms. Everything appeared normal. She went back to Chapman's room. The EEG machine sat silent, and she wondered if she had dreamt its bold scribbling.

She bit her lower lip and decided not to mention anything in the night log, figuring the scribbling was an anomaly caused by the electrical surge. She would check the machine later for damage.

27

Madison Park

*mall talk should be nondenominational and, especially, nonlethal. It
should center on weather, pets, trivia — what only the speaker knows
the answer to or cares about — and weird science. Absolutely, family
should be banned from the small talk list, especially at the dinner table, to
guarantee an event of safe, mindless conviviality.*

Not this night.

The evening at home started harmlessly with Hagler and Pamela
shaking hands and exchanging the usual cliché banalities.

The festivities slid downhill from there.

Hagler knew about Cassandra meeting me for lunch. It didn't
take a genius to figure out she wanted me to accompany her to the
abortion clinic. As I said, Hagler was a putz, but also smart.

So, of course, he brought it up. I won't bore you with the details
except to say Pamela kept the wine chilled with her eyes and voice.
Hagler, oblivious to any social cues as well as my repeated attempts to

change the subject, kept crying over Cassandra while insinuating I was the bad guy in her decision.

The meal ended when the cook cleared the main course but didn't bring in a dessert. Pamela showed Hagler the den. "The couch is very comfortable," she told him. She left without a flicker of a smile in my direction when I said, "I'll be right up."

"Thanks," I said sarcastically to Hagler after Pamela closed the door with a frosty slam.

Hagler clinked his Heineken against mine. "Back at you." The goat turd meant it.

I had taken my last Risperdal four hours earlier, so I was able to resist the urge to pluck his blue eyeballs from his graying head and shove them down his evil throat. I managed a charitable smile and generously let his evening of *mal faux pas* go.

He was staring into the gas log fireplace and missed my Oscar-winning performance. He took a long draw of beer and set the bottle on the fireplace's rock mantle next to a sixteenth-century astrolabe globe Pamela picked up in a flea market outside of Venice. "I'm stumped, Jack."

If he brought up Cassandra again, I'd shove his face into the flames.

Instead, he said, "I don't know why we think murders have been committed. Nothing suggests foul play except the loss of blood." He looked at me blankly. "Where's the human element to make it murder?"

"You think it's Sasquatch like Mickey and Mack?"

"You got a better explanation?" he shot back. "Look, no way a person could have killed these guys. No technology exists to drain blood from a body that fast."

"You think it's the supernatural."

He shrugged. "It's as good an explanation as any."

"So, a vampire cult sucked the blood out of our victims then turned into bats to escape detection?"

"It's as good an explanation as any."

I put my beer next to his. "You going to finish your drink?" Hagler asked. I shook my head. He downed the rest of his and picked up mine. I left him staring into blue-tipped flames.

Upstairs, Pamela had stayed up reading.

Shucking off my suit, I crawled into bed with her. I took it as a good sign she didn't object to me joining her. So, on the theory women want to talk things out, and true courage was facing my fear of having a knockdown, dragged-out fight with her that would leave me homeless, I said, "You're upset."

"Your never-wrong gut tell you that?" she snapped.

"You're holding the book upside down." She wasn't, but I thought I'd try the humor approach.

She shot my remark out of the air with a laser stare like an enemy UFO.

(Maybe you're interested in what two mature adults argue about in bed to see if it matches your own shit. I'm not interested in sharing.)

The conversation went back and forth until an early morning phone call mercifully ended it. Pamela growled softly against the intrusion, angry I would answer instead of continuing the talk we had started much earlier. The old line "It's work" didn't mollify her any.

Dispatch told me we had another triad killing in a case with no leads. The puzzle had grown ever more demanding, because I could find no way of solving it. The increasing possibility of the I-5 Dragons declaring war on the tongs didn't help. Nor did Uncle Lo's deadline with only two days left. But the threat of hostilities and crossing Uncle Lo paled to Pamela's disapproval. Angry eyes glared at me, and she hunkered down under the covers when I tried to hug her before I got out of bed.

I suppose I couldn't blame her any. What might have been a cozy dinner and a wonderful snuggle under the covers had been anything but. Feeling the way I did — like when my college girlfriend kicked me out of her dorm room — I carried my clothes and shoes downstairs and dressed in the foyer.

If I couldn't blame Pamela, Hagler was another thing altogether. Once dressed, I knocked on the door to the den, gleeful at the opportunity to wake him, only to discover the ME already dressed and ready to go.

"We've got another body," he said.

28

Columbia Center

Seattle's Columbia Center is a soaring tower of glass and steel that rises 937 feet and dwarfs every other building downtown. During the day, it draws a steady stream of visitors. Sightseers flock to the rooftop atrium to enjoy the panorama of Puget Sound backlit by the rainforest-shrouded mountainsides of the Olympic Peninsula. Professionals lease its offices, clients arrive for meetings and patrons fill its bars and restaurants. Jobbers navigate its corridors and gawkers gape at anything rising high into the air.

At 2:00 in the morning, the Center is all but deserted, the front entrance dimly lit and uninviting, while dark-sky lighting softly illuminates a brick courtyard sheltered from the street by curbside trees. It's the last place anyone would think of visiting, except on a dare, since security chases away anyone setting foot on the property unless they belong there. Yet, a few dozen fools a year — usually high school or college kids — are detained and handed off to the first Seattle cruiser to answer security's call.

Not tonight.

. . .

Courtyard lights were shattered, and CSI hadn't arrived with the klieg lights. We had to inspect everything with phone flashlights. It wasn't a perfect place to commit a murder. Guards toured the area every fifteen minutes, and full-spectrum, digital camera UV and IR ghost-hunting gear (you read it right — ghost hunting) covered every line of sight in the atrium. And, yeah, you're way ahead of me — the security cameras filmed a bright flash before going offline for one minute.

When Hagler and I arrived together on the scene, his techs, the Sparrowhawk brothers, were standing over the corpse taking selfies.

Their antics didn't bother me as much as when they turned the body over. I blinked back surprise. Beneath the vivid bruising on both cheeks and around the eyes was Benny Yee, William Chen's bodyguard and the guy who'd filmed the Dragon's leader dropping a wad of cash into my coat pocket. The money was still there, by the way, burning a proverbial hole; I really didn't know what to do with it.

I knew I had to get Benny's phone before somebody put two and two together and blamed me for his murder. I pulled on a pair of latex gloves and said to Hagler, "Let's see what he's got on him." I went through his pockets. Wallet, butterfly knife — the I-5 Dragons' weapon of choice — a pack of Dentyne gum, a couple of Trojans — apparently, he expected something more enjoyable this evening than having the blood sucked out his body — and a ball of lint. Seriously. Chinese are great collectors, and Benny Yee collected lint. I hoped it was pocket lint and not the navel variety.

The phone wasn't on him. Of course, it wouldn't be easy. Chen probably had it at one of his stash houses or on him. I handed Hagler the wallet.

He checked the ID before bagging it.

I said, "Don't bother, Mel. It's Benny Yee... one of William Chen's bodyguards."

Hagler's eyes widened. "What's an I-5 Dragon doing here? It's way outside their turf."

"Could be a body dump. Chen doesn't want the publicity in Chinatown. It's bad for business."

"You going to ask him?"

"As soon as we're done here."

Hagler shrugged. "Go on. I'll finish up."

"You sure?"

"What you see is what you get. Another vampire killing."

Mickey and Mack laughed, and I heard "Sasquatch" again. I didn't take it personally. Right now, the Sparrowhawk twins' guess was as good as mine.

Hagler's phone pinged. So did mine. I read the text. Another body had dropped. This one in Chinatown. William Chen wasn't going to tell us anything.

29

Chinatown

The cobblestoned alley behind the Flowing Water Benevolent Society, like every other alley in Chinatown, is filled with trash. You need hepatitis and tetanus vaccinations just to enter, let alone poke around the tangled chaos of rusty, serrated tin can lids, crushed plastic bottles, used diapers, malodorous secretions, foul discharges, and rotting offal looking for clues.

The society, however, is clean. It's been around for 160 years, the second oldest of the Seattle tongs, the one least involved with crime, and the richest of all the tongs, too. Made up of artisans, construction workers, and stay-at-home moms, they pool their small savings for investments. They never do anything terribly illegal, and compared to the I-5 Dragons, they're a Cub Scout troop. Which leads to a boatload of splendid irony.

Officer Sandra Liu was unwinding police tape between light poles to keep out gawkers when Hagler and I rolled up on the scene. Captain Billy's body was sprawled against a dumpster overflowing with food scraps from the next-door pad thai noodle restaurant. It was William

Chen's joss to die in an alley, thrown out of life like the trash. A fitting end, in my humble opinion.

The alley's only light was busted. Maybe, like the other three killings, it had exploded from some unknown force creating an overload. And maybe the storeowner just didn't give a crap about security or safety. And forget about security cams. Sure, the Flowing Water Benevolent Society was generally lawful, but they didn't want anyone recording what happened outside their doors at midnight, or any other time — discretion being the better part of staying out of prison.

Hagler tsked, took out his phone, and snapped a selfie with the body. Yeah, it was a quirk of his, but I couldn't say anything. After all, without the Risperdal, I'd have a lot of quirks... weird quirks. When he finished, I donned gloves and went through Chen's pockets. I'd seen homeless with more on them than this guy. No phone, no wallet, no weapon — just another bloodless corpse, face punched a couple of dozen times, a mile away from his gangbanger buddy. The connection was obvious, but not the distance. Maybe Sheila Cummings could work some of her CSI magic and figure out how it all related.

Hagler was finishing a call to the Sparrowhawk brothers. "Screw protocol. Swing by here and pick up the other body, then head to the morgue."

"You're not worried about messing up my case by contaminating evidence?" I asked.

Hagler shrugged. "What evidence?"

He was right about that. Four crime scenes, and nothing.

"Besides, who cares if these gangbangers are dead, Jack. I say good riddance."

"The last gang war left eighteen people dead, thirteen of them civilians."

Hagler shrugged again. I guessed the shit going down with Cassandra really preyed on his wits, so I let it pass. He was a good ME, and divorce can rattle anyone. Especially when you married out of your league like Hagler had. He was balding, wore glasses — not the hip kind, but granny glasses from the sixties — and dressed frumpily in a broadcloth frock coat from an era too long gone to be retro chic.

Still, Cassandra had seen something in him other women didn't. Maybe that something had faded, and she wanted out. Then again, maybe I didn't want to believe the abortion was the only thing rushing her toward divorce.

I left him and approached Officer Liu. "What are the natives telling you?" I pointed at the gathering crowd.

"The usual," she said. "Nobody wants to talk, and those I pressed said they saw nothing. They couldn't wait to get away from me."

I grimaced. "Shit. Seattle isn't the old country. The police can be trusted here." It was an old rant of mine.

Liu didn't let it slide. "It's a cultural thing not a geographical one."

"So?"

"You're Irish."

"What does that mean?"

"Your family had troubles during the Easter Uprising with bad coppers."

I waved the comment away. "Christ, that was a hundred years ago."

"Would you trust a London cop?"

"Not on my life."

"So it is with Chinese," she said. "We've had three thousand years of experience to know just how bad government and its enforcers can be."

"But you're a cop," I said, surprised at her attitude.

Liu frowned, and the bitterness in her voice startled me. "My family disowned me. They won't even invite me to birthday parties or weddings. My parents only call me to fix traffic tickets, which I don't do, by the way."

"So...?"

She gnawed at her lower lip a moment. "So, you're not going to get any leads from the Chinese community. You're going to have to seek them elsewhere." She jerked her thumb over her shoulder.

I looked in the direction Liu pointed. Standing in the crowd behind the police tape was Khoury. The psychic gave me a look equal to that of my third-grade teacher, Mrs. Rosenstein, just before sending me to the principal's office.

Liu smiled.

"What?" I said.

"Careful. You've got a girlfriend at home."

No secrets in Copland. "I don't play the field," I protested.

"Then you'd better watch your back."

"You know something?" I pressed.

Liu snickered. "I'll spell it out for you with one-syllable words. She's at the crime scenes and at your desk. The looks she gives you aren't about psychic crap."

"Psychic is two syllables."

"So is psycho."

I sputtered something incoherent and left the patrolwoman laughing.

Walking toward Khoury, I realized for the first time she was short, but she didn't appear short. She had a presence, what *Entertainment Tonight* called the "it factor." But it was more than a catchphrase that had Officer Liu snickering and me intrigued. 'Exotic' objectified her and didn't tell even half the story. Maybe it was the whole package — thin nose, high cheekbones, full lips, and coal-dark eyes that held the flashing brilliance of intelligence far greater than mine — that had me viewing her in a new light.

I stopped inside the police tape. "What are you doing here?" was too cliché to ask, so I did the next best thing — I glared at her.

"Good to see you too, detective," she said in lilting, Lebanese-accented English.

She clutched her EMF, but I wasn't ready to let her stroll around the crime scene, especially with CSI and the ME doing their things. Dawn was an hour away. "Look, we're busy here. Meet me at the precinct at nine. We'll talk then."

"What's wrong with now?"

A lot of things intruded on "now" — the oncoming dawn was washing out the blue-black darkness of the night sky; I hadn't slept, up half the night at two crime scenes; I was hungry and hadn't had coffee or my morning dose of Risperdal yet; my eyes jerked around as if trying to follow bats catching insects; my mom's health; plus, I still hurt from the revelation that Cassandra didn't marry me because a psychic told her not to.

"Nine o'clock," I repeated. "I have someone else to talk to."

30

Good Luck Noodle House

The oldest records of the ancient Chinese art of divination describe it as a measure for "solving doubts." Chinese soothsayers employ lots of techniques, such as face and palm reading. My personal favorite is Tai Yi Shen Shu — the Great Yi God Calculation — used to launch wars. What better way to start a fight than to have some soothsayer tell you the gods proclaim it's an auspicious day to kill your enemies?

Auntie Toy's method of telling the future comes from the I Ching, an ancient Chinese text and the oldest of the Chinese classics. The I Ching uses a type of divination called cleromancy, which produces random numbers. Six numbers between six and nine are turned into a hexagram, which is looked up in the I Ching to forecast your fortune.

If you haven't guessed by now, I don't believe in this ethereal, astral realm, divination crap. But the Chinese do, and these murders were going down on their turf.

Auntie Toy had to be in her seventies, though no one knew for sure. She was a spare, birdlike woman with pale skin and dark eyes that missed nothing. She wore a brocaded green silk jacket over a green satin cheongsam that reached to her ankles. A tall beauty in her youth, she had been shortened by time, but her back was still straight, and she radiated a charismatic aura that entranced everyone who met her.

Myth and rumor said she came over from China as a young girl after Mao's Red Guard shipped her parents to the countryside for re-education in the late 1950s. She supposedly took the name of San Francisco's legendary Chinese madam, Ah Toy, who arrived in California in the 1850s and became the state's first multimillionaire. Auntie Toy claimed to be related and told everyone she started her career in Seattle the same way, when she landed in Elliot Bay on a smuggler's boat in June 1959.

I knew the truth. Ah "Auntie" Toy had been born Elizabeth Chee to a family who emigrated legally from Hong Kong to Vancouver, British Columbia in 1946 before the Mainland turned communist. Twenty years later, she had escaped an arranged marriage by fleeing Canada to Seattle and opened a brothel under the guidance of Uncle Lo. One brothel became two. Massage parlors followed and later strip joints. The two had become rich together. Rumor said Uncle Lo was the father of her eldest daughter.

I had no idea what Auntie Toy was so insistent on telling me outside of the usual psychic crap. But sitting in the back booth of the Good Luck Noodle House with the fragrance of jasmine tea rising from delicate porcelain cups that should have been in a museum somewhere, I knew Uncle Lo and her were serious, and I had better take them seriously. Besides, Uncle Lo practically ordered me to see his favorite soothsayer, an offer I dared not refuse given his subtle threats against the Police Brotherhood.

Their drawn, humorless faces didn't stop me from letting them know I was displeased at being ordered here, however. "So, Auntie Toy, after years of selling harmless fortunes to gullible tourists, Uncle Lo tells me you're into chasing ghosts."

"If you paid more attention to the spirit world, you wouldn't be in this mess," she snapped back in Mandarin.

Uncle Lo intervened. "Jack, we are all very worried. Five I-5 Dragon members dead with no leads and one of them William Chen... the leader. If you don't find the killer soon, it could lead to a war, as well as a fight against the police. This would be bad for business... everyone's business."

He held my gaze for several heartbeats, and I could feel the desperation in him. "All right," I said and listened without enthusiasm as Auntie Toy regaled me with five minutes of boring shit on the beauty and perfection of the *I Ching*.

"And this all leads up to what?" I asked, leaning back against the booth's side.

"The *I Ching* forecasted that the murders would be the work of a ghost out for revenge."

I rolled my eyes, and no, it wasn't the tardive dyskinesia. "Thanks for the revelation, but I already know the motive," I said, not bothering to stifle the yawn that had been building since I sat down.

Auntie Toy's sloe eyes narrowed, and she said frostily, "I can see why you're the Seattle Police Department's rising *star*."

In Mandarin, the word *star* has the same sound and tone as *gorilla*. I would have responded similarly, but Uncle Lo shook his head ever so slightly. I clamped down on what might have been one of my most subtle insults and pasted on a polite expression.

Auntie Toy wasn't fooled. Her stare bored into me. "Pay attention, Darvesh."

The use of my first name startled me. Maybe she meant to appeal to the Punjabi side of my heritage to make me feel more Asian and therefore receptive.

She reached into her jacket pocket and pulled out a red velvet pouch. Red is a lucky color in China. Untying the drawstring, she emptied the contents onto the table. Forty rectangular terra cotta clay tiles, each about one inch by two inches, slapped against the fading red Formica. Each tile, shaped like a domino, had a hexagram impressed on each side — the *I Ching* hexagrams used to make a divination. Each line in a hexagram has its own explanation, which the soothsayer clarifies using the *I Ching* as a guide.

(Hexagrams are like casting entrails, though a lot less messy and not nearly as entertaining as a tarot reading.)

"Choose six," she said.

"I thought you were supposed to pull them out one at a time without looking," I said, mostly to show her I knew a thing or two or three about her brand of hocus-pocus.

"This is your future. More importantly, you need to believe, so that when the time comes, you will not hesitate to act."

"That sounds ominous," I said, grinning.

"Choose," she ordered, her mien as stony as the restaurant's slate floor.

I chose blindly, shifting my gaze from Auntie Toy to Uncle Lo with each tile, until the six were separated from the others.

Black eyes, seemed to have no light shining out of them, stared at my face, and Auntie Toy swept the remaining tiles to the side. She then pushed one forward — a long bar above two shorter ones above another long bar followed by two more sets of short bars above a long bar. She placed a second tile end to end, forming a row. It mirrored the first.

For the first time since we sat down, Auntie Toy's attitude softened. "Nothing has changed," she said wistfully, not to me but Uncle Lo. His face paled, and he squeezed her hand.

"And that's bad?" I asked, still smiling.

"I had hoped with these last killings something had changed, and none of us would have to endure what follows." Without waiting for me to reply, she placed a third tile after the second, followed by a fourth and fifth until they stretched across the table toward me like an arrow pointing at my heart. She snapped the sixth one into place with such a flourish it banged through the quiet restaurant like a pistol shot.

She grimaced at the final pair of hexagrams and shook her head. Uncle Lo turned away, but not before I saw a great sadness in his eyes.

Hexagrams were supposed to show how yin and yang worked together to illuminate the future. To me, they were simple tiles with full and broken lines that signified superstition. Still, the smile drifted from my face, and I asked, perhaps too sharply, "What?"

"The killer you seek will find you first."

I felt my Glock riding on my hip, and my smile partially returned. "Good. Bring him on."

"You won't be able to stop him," she said.

Maybe I should have been cautious, but I didn't believe in any of her hocus-pocus crap. I was here to assuage Uncle Lo's concerns and to stop him from outing the Police Tong. "What's a ghost killer look like anyway?"

"His mind is very powerful. He can travel the astral plane and will not stop until every I-5 Dragon in Seattle is killed. He will kill anyone who gets in his way."

"Sure, sure, but what's he look like?"

She shook her head.

I sighed. "Of course. Thanks all the same, but I need a description if I'm going to stop this guy before he kills again."

Uncle Lo whispered to her in a dialect I didn't understand. She answered in a tone that suggested I was as feeble minded as a monkey. I resisted the urge to tell her I wasn't as stupid as I looked and waited for her to continue.

Auntie Toy took a sip of tea. "I don't know what he looks like today."

Maybe I was as stupid as I looked, or at least I must have appeared that way. All I could muster was, "I don't understand."

"His mind projects an image of what he was before a great tragedy struck his family — built like the gods, with black hair, straight nose, high cheekbones, cleft chin, and bright blue eyes."

The description, down to the family, fit Andrew Chapman, as if he were capable of sitting at the table with us. I didn't bother to tell her the ghost she described was currently brain dead in a coma at Greenbrier Nursing Home, where it was impossible for him to sit up let alone do the murders.

"And just how do I find a phantom that murders his victims by draining the blood out of them?" I asked with all the politeness I could muster.

"You must be careful," she said. "I won't be able to protect you."

I almost laughed at her concern, but hard lines of fate had returned to her face, and she wasn't kidding. "I'll be fine, Auntie Toy."

She frowned and said something to Uncle Lo in the same strange dialect.

The old man clapped his hands, and a waiter appeared carrying a silver serving dish, which he set down on the table between the two of us. Lo waited until the kid disappeared into the kitchen before lifting the cover. The tray held ten, five-ounce smuggler bars of gold.

I hid my shock by sipping tea and doing a quick calculation of the wealth plunked down in front of me like an unassuming side dish at a banquet. The gold market in Europe listed it at USD 2,035 per ounce two nights ago according to Pamela. $101,750. It made William Chen's offer a pittance.

Lo waited for the astonishment to drain from my face. "When you find the murderer, you receive the gold," he said bluntly, not bothering with innuendo. It was unlike the old man, which, along with the gold, meant he and the other tongs must be very worried. "Listen to Ah Toy, Jack," he said, using her formal name.

The gold had taken all the banter out of the conversation, so I sipped more tea and thought of Khoury, who I was to meet in an hour at the precinct. She hawked the same line as Auntie Toy. It seemed everybody, even my captain, was bent on herding me toward the supernatural. It didn't make any sense. Ghosts can't kill people. They certainly can't drain them of blood. Yet $100,000 in gold showed Uncle Lo and Auntie Toy were deadly serious.

31

West Precinct

*P*olice television shows and movies often portray a shining moment of insight sparked by some absurd coincidence as the catalyst to an arrest of the bad guys, or, more likely, a shootout where more ammo is expended on screen than at all the firing ranges in Seattle on a given day — which reminds me of a quote by the legendary creator of Perry Mason, Erle Stanley Gardner. When asked why, in a gun battle, his hero never took down the bad guy until the last round was fired, Gardner answered, "At three cents a word, every time I say 'Bang' in the story, I get three cents. If you think I'm going to finish the gun battle while my hero still has fifteen cents worth of unexploded ammunition in his gun, you're nuts."

Khoury wasn't waiting when I walked into the precinct, and I had a chance to settle my thoughts on a morning filled with two dead bodies and otherworldly strangeness. Only, as I trudged up the stairs at the station house, my thoughts whipsawed back and forth, to and fro, up and down, inside and out. Auntie Toy had rattled me with her talk of a psychopathic, supernatural killer in my future. (Say that sentence out loud if you want to know just how ridiculous it sounds.)

Still, I was rattled. The sad earnestness of Toy's *I Ching* reading and Lo's disconsolate acceptance that the future could not be changed had unsettled my glib protests against their paranormal explanation of the killings.

On the other hand, after the hit on Chen, I really didn't have time to waste on paranormal tales of a ghostly bogeyman killing off gang-bangers at a rate faster than they could be replaced. Nor could I indulge cleverly constructed theories of the astral plane to spark a breakthrough in my investigation and point to the killer. The I-5 Dragons wouldn't wait. Twenty of them would drive around in cars until they found the dumb bastards they figured were responsible and waste them.

Still, my ever-reliable gut, which dealt only in real-world explanations of mysteries, betrayed me, shouting that Auntie Toy and Khoury had to be onto something. Too much weird, supernormal bullshit surrounding these killings had turned them into something far past ordinary homicides. With the usual flesh-and-blood suspects not readily available, I was desperate enough to follow up any lead no matter how bizarre to my way of thinking. And if somehow it did turn out to be a psycho-ghost it would be a first for my career. I didn't let my thoughts go down the path of how to arrest something I couldn't see. Ectoplasmic handcuffs weren't department issue.

I fell back into my chair, sorely needing a shot of tequila and a cigarette... both of which would screw me up worse than the Risperdal. I would just have to suffer.

Khoury came into the squad room escorted by Sandra Liu. "Visitor for you," she said with a wink.

Bite me.

Liu must have read my mind, because she laughed and flipped me the bird as she walked away.

Khoury's headscarf was pale blue today, and she wore red

lipstick and dark eye shadow. Very Western for a woman who came from a culture that frowned on women who drew attention to themselves with make-up. It also made her attractive and distracting. I wondered if she were doing it on purpose to throw me off my game.

"What do you need?" I asked in as professional a tone as I could.

"Access to the crime scene," she answered.

"So you can do your thing with your EMF."

"The sooner the better. The residual energy diminishes as time passes."

"And you know this, how?"

"I told you, detective, I have a PhD in physics."

"The study of electromagnetism and optics... I remember."

"Whoever is committing these murders also has extensive knowledge of neuroscience and Earth's geomagnetic field." She never took her gaze from me.

"So, our killer is an expert... like yourself.... Probably has a PhD also."

"Most likely," she answered straight as if not getting the irony.

"How did you end up studying this field?" I didn't call bullshit, though I thought it.

"I was a researcher at the American University of Beirut." She paused as if I should know what that means. I did but waited for her to say it. (Yeah, I can be a dick.) "It is one of the most prestigious universities in the Middle East," she added.

"And yet, here you are in Seattle chasing ghosts for a living. Why the change?"

"Others did not appreciate my research, so I came to the US where people are more open-minded."

"Some are.... Some are closed doors."

She lowered her gaze, but not before I read her eyes. She had told only a portion of the story, leaving out the part, I figured, that somehow connected to the case . But as good as my hunch was, I still needed proof. And the only way to get it was to lead her out on a limb.

"All right. You can visit the crime scene and do whatever you do with that fancy gadget of yours."

"Thank you." She got up and waited, her taut posture saying she expected me to escort her.

"Oh, not with me. I have too much other work to keep up with at present." I really did. My other cases weren't going away anytime soon, and I had to check in on them. "I'll have Patrolwoman Liu take you to the crime scene."

"Of course," she said in a tone that didn't hide her disappointment.

"I want a full report on what you find," I added.

"As soon as I have made my determination." She extended her hand, and I shook it. Soft skin, strong bones.

She left. I phoned McCrory at the desk and told him to get Sandra Liu to show Khoury the latest crime scene. Hanging up, I went to the window and waited. She exited the building with Liu, who gave me the finger again as they headed toward her patrol car. They left the station toward Chinatown. And right behind them, the tan Volvo followed. The distance wasn't great, and I got a good look at the driver — Middle Eastern profile; heavy beard stubble and dark skinned.

Bingo, I thought. The guy who followed Khoury the other night was mixed up in it somehow. I called McCrory and asked for Liu's cell phone number. I shot her a text to be on the lookout for a tan Volvo and asked her to get a picture of the driver if she could without spooking him.

Maybe I could catch a break in the mystery of the triad killings by uncovering Khoury's connection to the case.

I didn't get much work done the rest of the day. The ME's report on Chen and his bodyguard was a forensic dead end: death by exsanguination... no DNA under the fingernails... no hair or fibers on the clothing... no fingerprints... no blood at the scenes. A whole lot of nada. Whoever killed these guys had apparently shrink-wrapped himself before committing the murders.

Running down statements from witnesses during the canvass was just as useless. I listened to people say they saw nothing in ten different dialects and languages. I also ran into a joker who answered questions in Klingon. He was a *p'takh*.

Late in the afternoon, the pile of paper on my desk hadn't gotten any smaller, but I did receive some news of the this-raises-more-questions-than-answers variety. Liu had been able to get a clear picture of the tan Volvo's license plate and the driver. His name was Mahir Khoury, a Lebanese national in Seattle on a tourist visa. According to the FBI, he was a doctor in Beirut, unassociated with any terrorist groups, and — get this — he was Khoury's younger brother. Why was he following his sister around? And why had she lied to me about knowing him? But getting answers to those questions would have to wait.

At 5:00, my shift ended, and I was beat. I didn't relish the idea of home and Pamela's coolness. I had phoned her twice, and she hadn't picked up. Fortunately, I didn't have to go right away. I called Hagler and told him I'd pick him up at the ME's office around midnight. I had an errand to run first. Mel didn't complain. He had a free place to stay, after all.

Malvern stopped by my desk, a red vine of licorice turning in his hand. "You working with the Khoury woman?" he asked, with the expectation I'd better say yes.

"As ordered, but I gotta tell you, there's something hinky with her, boss." I told him about the brother following her.

Malvern bit off a piece of licorice and shook the ragged end at me. "Brother, *shmother*. You haven't any leads, and she's the only person who has an idea of where to look for answers. You will work with her."

I hid my lack of enthusiasm with a smile and a salute.

32

Chinatown
The Buddha Diner

Whispers of a secret tong within the Seattle Police Department have been around for at least two decades. According to the rumors, a brotherhood of select police officers runs Chinatown like a business. They control gambling and prostitution — the so-called harmless crimes. They also make sure the district is clear of any drugs and is safe for civilians.

Whenever anyone brings up this rumor, I tell them flat out that if true, the tong would be raking in millions a year, and the perpetrators would be driving Lamborghinis. Yet, there isn't a cop in Chinatown who doesn't struggle to make his or her mortgage or put food on the table. If these cops are so rich, how come they're like the other 99 percent of Seattle who can barely manage to live here?

That generally ends the talk, as I intended. What I don't tell them is that the Police Tong members are smart, and the leader is smart too.

I climbed the worn back stairs of Chinatown's Buddha Diner. In the front, the Asian deli served the best Thai food in the city, and Seattleites often lined up around the corner just to take noodle bowls home. Tonight, business was almost dead — no line and only a few tables filled.

Not a good sign, I thought. *The threat of a war with the I-5 Dragons is bad for business, bad for the Police Tong's income.*

I glanced at the alley's surveillance cams, unafraid. Corporal Kee in SPD's computer crimes division had hacked the camera's server to play an innocuous loop during the meetings; the comings and goings of the Police Tong were never recorded.

The palm lock on the back door opened to my touch. I entered and saw the inner core already gathered around the large wooden table in the center of the room. Nine men, all from the West Precinct, all Asian, all sworn by blood oaths to protect the tong and keep the Chinatown-International district safe.

I took my customary place at the head of the table as the high dragon. Yeah, it had been my idea. I recruited these guys my first year as a detective. I had studied their records and found the men who would serve the city first and not be tempted to use the money for personal gain.

Unlike police tongs in Hong Kong, Taiwan, and Macau, we took nothing for ourselves except the occasional dinner out with the family. All the money from the operations went into a special fund, or we gave it to charity. The fund sent kids to college. Half the children of the men in this room were doctors, lawyers, or programmers. Asians had a long-term view of families — the latter generations have to live better, contribute to the family, and help the next generation. It was how I got these men to agree to never use the money for themselves. And I was sure none of them would. If someone got into trouble, the others would come to his aid.

Tea had already been poured, and a plate of Chinese appetizers sat untouched in the center of the table. The fragrances of jasmine, savory barbecue pork, and honeyed prawns competed with the sharp flavors of pad thai and red curry coming from the restaurant below. The others waited until I placed several pieces on a small plate with slender bamboo chopsticks.

Corporal Kee spoke as soon as I had taken a sip and raised my cup appreciatively at the aromatic taste. "Rumor says the old-time tongs are offering fifty *taels* of gold to whoever finds the vampire killers responsible for these murders and ends their miserable lives." A *tael* was an ancient Chinese monetary unit fixed at 50 grams or 1.75 ounces.

The Kee family owned a teahouse — where they served traditional Cantonese small foods called *yum cha*, "drink tea meals" — that provided the food we ate tonight. They also ran two laundromats, a bakery, and a chain of payday check-cashing operations. They were all legitimate businesses run by his two younger brothers, who had graduated with MBAs from Harvard. No one could be part of the Police Brotherhood Tong unless they and their families were completely within the law. The Kees were doing very well, but an extra $175,000 in untraceable gold wouldn't hurt.

"It's ten smuggler bars," I corrected him. "Lo showed me the reward this afternoon. And the killers aren't vampires. They're men, flesh and blood, the same as you and me."

"$101,750 is still a lot of money," Kee said almost breathlessly. The others agreed with vigorous nods.

"Stop drooling, corporal. I don't have to remind you these murders are bad for Chinatown and therefore bad for us. It's important we find the killers quickly."

Sergeant Akama leaned back in his chair, lips puckered, in thought. A large Chinese American with a shaved head, dark brows, and a double chin, he sweated heavily in the late August heat. Though born in the United States, he had been homeschooled until ten and still spoke with an accent, his words peppered with Cantonese idioms. "*Ayeeyah!* It's still a lot of money. But not enough to catch a *jiangshi*—" His voice trailed off and he couldn't suppress a shudder. *Jiangshi* literally meant "hopping vampire" or "hopping zombie."

"No such thing, Sergeant Akama," I admonished the older officer.

"My auntie disagrees," the big man countered.

I looked at the solemn faces of the other men around the table, each echoing the sergeant's opinion. They were decorated Asian-American officers, all of whom had put their lives on the line to protect civilians from danger more than once in their careers. One didn't get to be a member of the Police Brotherhood Tong unless he was brave and selfless. I thought about Sandra Liu's assertion that Chinese mistrusted cops, even their own. Yet, I would put my life in the hands of any of these officers. Still, thousands of years of ingrained folklore and superstition could make them shiver.

"We have to stop them, nonetheless," I said, not bothering to argue the validity of vampires and zombies. "Lean on your CIs. Somebody has to have seen something."

"What reward can we offer them?" Kee asked. The others leaned in, looking at me. I had to choose carefully and correctly. The incentive had to be enough to lure a CI to give up anything he knew about the I-5 Dragons and the Seattle tongs to stop a war, but not so much to cut into the substantial amount of money the lucky officer would earn if his CI broke the case wide open. "One tael," I said.

Kee nodded, and the others sat back, satisfied $3,500 was the perfect amount.

"On to other business," I announced.

Leung Po, a twenty-year career officer, who also worked as a CPA during tax season, opened the brotherhood's books. He kept meticulous records, down to the penny paid by each brothel owner and every gambling hall. mah-jongg and fan-fan were particularly heavy contributors, because Asians loved to gamble. In the ten years the tong had been operating, we had made over $5 million, safely tucked away in Grand Cayman accounts, and contributed four times that to Seattle charities. If anyone discovered the secret, we'd be in jail in a heartbeat. And yet, Chinatown was the safest place in Seattle... at least until someone had started killing off I-5 Dragon Triad members.

"All our revenues are down for the week," Po explained as each member inspected the amounts. "The vampire killer has scared off customers."

We all agreed leaning on the brothels and gaming halls for the usual financial contributions wasn't in the spirit of community policing. Besides, it was our job to keep the area free of crime, so visitors felt safe to enjoy the leisurely pursuits of flesh and gambling. It was only fitting we shared the misery.

33

Chinatown

A *sians generally look at bad things happening and good things happening and call it joss. It's sort of like fate, kismet, karma, and god's will all rolled into luck and fortune. You can have good joss or bad joss, depending which side of events you end up on. You can do lots of things to improve your joss — good work, bribing the gods, looking both ways when crossing the street, not walking down dark alleys. But when bad joss determines your number's up, it's up. Not that joss stops people from trying their hardest to avoid the grim reaper when he arrives at the door with a postage-due letter.*

The meeting ended when it always did, half an hour before midnight. Midnight was when Corporal Kee's digital loop reverted to the real view of the alley and the area around the Happy Good Luck Diner. We left singly or in pairs, never as a group, so we didn't draw attention. And we always took separate routes to our cars, which we had parked far enough away to not draw suspicion.

(Maybe you're wondering why I didn't insist the brotherhood

meet over Zoom or FaceTime or Jitsi so we didn't have to bother with looping the camera feeds or parking cars. Because using social media would paint a target on the tong's back, like Uncle Lo, I never wanted any recordings of what the brotherhood did. We couldn't risk being hacked or exposed to the press or the Seattle police commissioner's office. Though we paid to have friends in high places, the precaution only worked if we were discreet and anonymous. Social media is anything but.)

As usual, I was the last one out. Tonight, I had parked about half a mile away in an alley off South Washington, just beyond Kobe Park, a tranquil area honoring Seattle's sister city, Kobe, Japan. The park closed at 10:00.

My route took me past the Hing Hay pavilion. I thought of Willie Fong and hurried along. Once past its ominous foreboding, highlighted by the police tape still separating it as a crime scene, I slowed my pace and stopped worrying about vampire killers or bloodletting Sasquatch.

I thought of Cassandra and Pamela and what I would do if I had a chance to choose between them. I mean really choose. They were both incredible and so far out of my league I couldn't figure out why fate had given me the chance in the first and second place.

It hit me as I approached the alley: if choosing meant losing them both, I probably wouldn't get a third shot at the brass ring. I needed to be careful not to waste what choice I did have.

Usually, I didn't enter the alley directly but through a business owned by a buddy. He gave me a key and let me hang out inside after hours. He thought I was meeting someone for a tryst. Tonight, I was tired and didn't want to go through the work of opening and closing the place. Besides, some of the fear from Chinatown had crept into nearby neighborhoods, and the alley was deserted.

Benny Yee's brother, Fargo, didn't bother wearing a mask. Yeah, Fargo. It was a large family: eight sons, three daughters. Maybe they ran out of names. Unlike Benny, he was short, round, and wore glasses. A decade younger, Fargo wasn't a triad. He had wanted to join out of high school, but Benny forced him to go study medicine at the

University of Washington. Probably the only decent thing Benny had ever done in life. At least the I-5 Dragons weren't after me... yet. They would have sent half a dozen gangbangers at once.

Fargo hadn't come unarmed, though. A pair of butterfly knives glinted silver-blue under the alley's clear white light. The effortless way he twirled the blades told me he'd been practicing.

He sauntered toward me, as if out for an evening stroll with a girl-friend, a grim smile on his moon face. Security cams were pointed upward at the night sky. Fargo had done his homework.

"Fargo," I said. "Sorry to hear about your brother."

He frowned. Maybe it was my insincerity.

"Turn around and walk away now, and I'll forget you ever menaced a police officer."

He laughed. Felony menacing was the least he had planned.

The thought crossed my mind — *The idiot brought a knife to a gunfight.* When I reached for my Glock, the second guy grabbed me from behind.

An arm the size of my leg squeezed my neck so hard the skin burned. He had me in a sleeper hold, the lethal chokehold police departments across the country were prohibited to use by federal law. Yeah, ironic.

I had six seconds before I blacked out, then Fargo could do what-ever he wanted to me. I kicked my attacker's left knee. He grunted and loosened his grip. That was my opening, you'd think. So did I. But the big guy pulled me backwards off my feet before I could do more than take a sharp breath. He squeezed harder. Darkness rushed at me from the sides like a collapsing tunnel, leaving a narrow point of light like from an oncoming train hurtling toward me through the blackness.

I was having the strange thought I'd never get to choose between Pamela and Cassandra when the grip eased suddenly. Oxygen rushed to my brain. It hurt, like firecrackers exploding inside my skull.

I groped for my Glock. A hand gently touched my arm. "No need," a kind voice whispered.

My vision cleared. Fargo lay face down on the alley's cold bricks.

His knives had vanished. I spun around. The big guy who choked me lay on the cobblestones with his hands on his chest as if praying. "Are they dead?" I asked. Yeah, it was lame, but my head still pounded.

"Don't worry. They're sleeping." I recognized who the voice belonged to — Uncle Lo's nephew, Malcolm. My vision cleared, and the thundering explosions in my head reduced to a banging trashcan lid.

Malcolm Lo was my height, slimmer, with pink hair shaped into an arching wave toward his forehead. He wore a black t-shirt and faded blue jeans. He shook my hand. "My uncle desires for you to stay healthy."

"Naturally." I took a step and stumbled. Malcolm guided me to the rear bumper of my car. "Thanks. I'll just sit here until I get my wind back."

"Naturally." His head cocked, and he smiled. If he had a gold tooth, I'd swear he was a younger version of his uncle. "We're even."

"Until next time."

Malcolm shook my hand again and vanished.

I rested five minutes. My head stopped its shrill ache. I got into my car and left, but not before backing over the big guy's legs then driving over Fargo's left arm.

34

Madison Park/Ravenna Park

You ever get a wrenching, churning sensation in your gut like you're supposed to catch a plane but you're at the bus station? Like you know you should have ordered a toasted cheese sandwich, but you went for the fish linguini instead? Like you knew better than to listen to your cousin about that penny stock, but you went all in anyway?

Hagler's face was drawn and gray, but he didn't cry and stayed silent the entire drive from his office to home. I mentioned nothing about the attack. What could I say? Once inside, Hagler went directly to the den, grunting good night to me in a mangled growl as the door closed behind him.

I flipped on the lights to the staircase. Blankets and pillows had been piled on the bottom step.... Yeah, for me. I climbed the stairs to the second floor wearily and warily. I never figured Pamela would get this mad. She pitted her high-energy, cutthroat personality against the world's other commodity traders and made a spectacular living at it. She never once had begrudged me the hours I kept or the cases that kept me away from home.

I stood in the hallway outside the bedroom, my toes wriggling into the thick, wool carpet. Pamela made everyone take their shoes off at the front door, even the guys who delivered the new washing machine and dryer a month ago. My hand hesitated above the Victorian brass doorknob while I debated whether to go into the room, wake her, apologize and make amends, or sleep in the spare bedroom. *Carpe diem* was much less appealing at 1:00 in the morning. As the minutes ticked by, thoughts of my meeting with Cassandra intruded. I knew she'd never be part of my life the way I wanted. Even so, the fact I still had these feelings for her was what eventually kept me from opening the door.

If my own thoughts weren't enough to seize the moment, my cell phone nixed the opportunity. It was my father. He needed help, and mom wasn't around again.

I kissed my fingers and pressed them to the door. Maybe Pamela stirred. Maybe it was the sound of hope winging away through the open window. Either way, I left and wasn't so certain I would return.

Dad hadn't tried to get out of bed by himself this time around. I helped him to the bathroom and back into bed. We were silent until I went to turn out the light. "Why isn't your mom home?" His voice sounded both querulous and worried.

I stifled a shrug, which seemed the worse possible answer, and turned slowly, saying in all truthfulness, "I don't know, Pops. It's not like her to leave you alone."

His rheumy eyes teared, and his voice cracked. "She hasn't even come in the room to say good night in the past week."

A week, and I was just now hearing about Mom's absences. (Some son I am.) "I'll find out what's going on. I promise. You get some sleep."

It didn't take a detective to figure out Mama's sudden indifference to her husband's needs meant something was up with her. The only way to figure out what was going on was to confront her. I went downstairs to wait and fell asleep on the couch.

She didn't come home that night.

The only good thing about the long night — no one called me to another triad murder. Maybe the psycho-ghost had gotten tired of killing, or, more likely, the human killer needed to sleep once in a while.

At 6:00, I called Pamela. She didn't pick up. I told myself that with the European markets closing and the US markets opening, she must be busy. Yeah, right. Physicist Richard Feynman's famous quote came to mind: "The first principle is that you must not fool yourself — and you are the easiest person to fool." I left her half a dozen voice mails.

I hung out in the kitchen, making coffee and keeping an ear out for Pops — he slept soundly — until the morning caretaker showed up at 8:00. Luis Carlos. I had vetted him when he first came to work for my parents. The kid had a PhD in physiology, but home health care was the only job he could score in this economy. I asked if he could stay later today until my mom got home. He happily agreed. He and my dad spent a lot of time playing cribbage. He was also teaching Pops all the Spanish swear words the old man could learn.

Captain Malvern insisted his detectives be in the squad room at 9:00. I had plenty of time, so I made one last effort to find Mama. I pinged her on FaceTime. She answered.

"You didn't come home last night," I chided. Probably not the best way to get her to tell me what she'd been up to, but I worried not only about my father's care, but that something was terribly wrong with her.

"Don't start with me," she said. "I have a right to do what I want."

"You're married and have a husband who needs care."

She waved the question away as if it were nothing. "Him? He's faking it. The old fart can take care of himself." We talked this way for a while. She deflected every question, and every answer came back to her needs.

Finally, I'd had it and said, "Mama, what you're doing to Pops is wrong. You get home right now."

"Darv, I've done nothing wrong. Now be a good boy and keep a civil tongue in your head, or I won't make naan for you anymore."

She did make the best naan in the country. In high school, Liam McCrory would stay at my place just to eat a bucket load of it. All that aside, I had to get her some help. "Mama, you have to see a doctor. I think something's wrong."

"Darv, I love you, but your concern is wasted on me. I'm fine. Now run along to work." She ended the call with an abruptness that shouted, *Leave me alone!*

Minutes ticked by with no answer to how to get Mama the medical exam she needed. Then Cassandra's advice came back: *Bring the doctor to her.*

I pinged the family physician on FaceTime. He was a retired internist but still took care of some former patients. "The ones I can't say no to," he once explained to me. Fortunately, Pops and Mama were at the top of his list.

Dr. Herschel answered on the second ring. He appeared on the tiny screen just as I remembered him — droll, moon-shaped face, glasses, long earlobes like the Buddha. He remembered me and what I did for a living and asked about the triad murders. It was a reminder that work beckoned, so I didn't slog through small talk. I told him about my mom's sudden onset of bizarre behavior.

His lips pushed forward in a puzzled O. "When did this start?"

"A week ago maybe. Pops isn't certain."

"And all of a sudden, she's leaving without a care in the world as if not even married to your father?"

"That's what Pops says."

"She comes home?"

"In the mornings, I guess. I don't really know."

Dr. Herschel tapped a dirt-stained finger against his lips. In the background, I could see he was outside in the garden. A sigh seemed to roll through him. "Find her. Have her home tonight at 6:00. I'll stop by. And Jack," his eyes narrowed to slits of intense concern, "it's crucial she be there."

"I'll make certain she is," I promised.

"Good. And don't worry, Jack. I'm sure it's nothing serious." He waved, and his image disappeared.

I stared uncomprehendingly at the Seattle skyline pic on the phone's home screen. *Don't worry* was the exact opposite of how I interpreted the underlying tension in Dr. Herschel's questions.

Malvern called. Fortunately, it was only audio. The captain staring at me with a swizzle of red licorice hanging from his mouth wasn't how I wanted to start my day as a detective. His angry voice was quite enough. "Doyle, get your ass to the station. Dr. Khoury is waiting to see you."

I checked on Pops. Luis had just laid down a twenty-point hand and skunked him in their first round of cribbage. "*Mierda!*" Pops cried.

I didn't need to speak Spanish to know what he meant. "You'll get him the next game, Pops."

"Damn straight, I will. Deal 'em, Luis," he ordered, sounding more like his usual irascible self.

The young caretaker grinned.

I patted Pops on the shoulder. With Luis here, I put the problem of my parents into a little compartment in my mind and concentrated on Dr. Khoury and the triad killings. She had a lot to answer for — such as why she didn't recognize her own brother.

35

West Precinct

I t really does rain constantly in Seattle from fall to the end of spring. You can look it up. The city on the shores of Puget Sound averages 37.49 inches of rain a year, with the most on record — 55.14 inches — coming in 1950.

You might claim, rightly, the amount doesn't even come close to Mt. Waialeale on Kauai in Hawaii, which gets 450 inches of rain a year, or Ketchikan, Alaska with over twelve feet of rain a year and a paltry eighty-six days of sunshine.

Still, in Seattle, it seems to rain all the time from September to June. That's because it doesn't fall as hard as it does in Ketchikan or Hawaii. The gray overcast and drizzle sweep over the city so constantly, after a while, it seeps through the skin until the body starts to creak and freeze up as if rusting from the inside.

Citizens here use umbrellas the way Arizonans use sunglasses. They even have umbrellas attached to leashes for their pets. Hell, Seattleites celebrate an annual bumbershoot festival over Labor Day weekend which, appropriately, is when the rainy season traditionally starts in Seattle with the finality of a curtain falling in the theater.

. . .

I stopped outside the precinct's glassed-in entryway to watch a bevy of clouds scud across Seattle's skyline. Not enough to herald rain but an ill omen, nonetheless. The rainy season approached rapidly, and I needed to focus if I was ever to solve the triad murders before the bright blue of summer turned to the gray foreboding of fall.

The Risperdal bottle felt heavy in my pocket. Though the drug allowed me to act like most people, it interfered with the total concentration I dedicated to mastering problems. Maybe halving the dose would help... or going off it completely. I had done that before, but Cassandra had been there to pick up the pieces and put me back together again.

I sighed, both for and against the thought, resisted the urge to give the clouds, the city, and the cases the finger and headed inside.

As soon as the doors closed behind me, McCrory gave me the sign not to go upstairs. Apparently, Malvern was on the warpath and had taken to eating more red licorice than the human body should be able to stand. The mayor had called, complaining tourism in China-town was way down the past few days because of the triad murders, saying the effect was spreading to other parts of the city. Considering tourists tended to shy away from Seattle during the rainy season's ten dreary months, I understood her honor's frustration and, by proxy, the captain's wish for the case to be solved quickly.

Mercifully, Khoury waited for me by the stairwell leading to the squad room, so I didn't have to endure Malvern's licorice-coated condemnation of my ineptitude. I asked McCrory to let him know I was escorting the psychic to the first crime scene, as he requested, with the hope of getting a break in the case.

We walked past her Mercedes, her ignoring my gaze darting every which way, and me using my tardive dyskinesia to scan the area for the tan Volvo. It wasn't around. That didn't mean Khoury's brother wasn't following her.

Once in my car, I decided not to grill her about their relationship. I wanted to see just how much rope she would take in to hang herself.

"So, did the EMF detector at the Columbia Center tell who the killer is?" I asked straight off.

She shook her head. "The readings were too faint to be of any use."

"And the alley behind the Flowing Water Benevolent Society?"

"Also no good."

"Then why go to Hing Hay Park? It's been three days since Willie Fong was killed. The signature must be gone by now."

"The rapidity with which the signal has degraded at the other two sites suggests the killer has become more subtle and is masking his energy signature, which shows he has a very good understanding of the body's electrical energy and how to use it on the astral plane."

"So, this so-called astral killer... this electromagnetic genius, is a he."

"I'm quite certain."

"Uh-huh," I said. My lack of enthusiasm made her frown.

"You're a skeptic."

I nodded, preferring silence to telling her my real feelings, that it was all bullshit.

"Astral travel is ancient and well documented in many cultures. The modern term, astral projection, was coined by the nineteenth-century British theosophist and women's rights activist, Annie Besant," Khoury explained, donning her professorial mode.

I drove and listened.... Really. Risperdal made me a good listener as opposed to the inappropriate "me, me, me" asshole I would be without it. Also, the tardive dyskinesia helped my driving. My eyes darted to every mirror. When the TD first started, it overwhelmed my seven-year-old brain and paralyzed me. I had several accidents on my bicycle before I learned to focus the drug's effect into a tool to provide my brain with a lightning-speed snapshot of everything going on around me. It was how I dodged the bullet that paralyzed McCrory.

"It is sometimes reported with dreams, meditation, and through various hallucinogenic and hypnotic means," Khoury said. "The etheric form of astral projection allows the practitioner to leave his body and visit anywhere in our physical world."

I managed to say without sneering, "No scientific evidence supports astral projection."

"Until now," Khoury said.

The TD kept me from slamming into the car in front of us. I collected myself and said, "So what kind of mad, evil genius should I be looking for?"

"I would say he has increased his brain's neural plasticity to the extent that he has many more neuronal connections than the average person."

"Can you put that in English a cop can understand?"

"His mind is so powerful, he has mastered the ability to connect his body's electromagnetic field to the Earth's geomagnetic field for astral projection."

Like Andrew Chapman, who would have been the prime suspect, except he was lying brain dead in a nursing home. I went to the next best choice. "Like you," I said directly, watching her for any tells that would give away her true interest in the I-5 Dragon killings.

"His powers are much greater than mine. I can use the EMF detector to sense the astral plane and great events happening within its realm. This man can actually manipulate the plane's energy to drain the blood from his victims."

The humble reply caught me by surprise. I changed the subject. "What do you hope to find at the Grand Pavilion?"

She bit her lower lip, then said, "I can't be certain, of course, but I'm hoping the first murder, the way he mutilated the body, was the one where he went all out and didn't bother masking his electromagnetic signature. Emanations from his etheric body may still linger."

"I'm a simple cop, remember? What does that mean?"

Her gaze narrowed, and the ends of her mouth curved up with a knowing smile. I got the feeling she saw right through my simple cop schtick. Maybe she even guessed my secret. Then she was all professorial again. "Electric current produces a magnetic field. We can visualize this magnetic field as a pattern of circular lines surrounding a wire, for example. Since the human body produces electrical energy—"

"Like a battery à la *The Matrix*," I interrupted.

"In a manner of speaking," she answered patiently. "Electricity is required for the nervous system to send signals throughout the body and to the brain, making it possible for us to move, think, and feel. As a result, every human being has a distinctive electromagnetic field pattern. It acts like a fingerprint. The EMF detector can track him once I get a clear reading."

"You can follow him back to his lair like a bloodhound on the scent of dirty socks?" (Yeah, I can be a real schmuck, and I don't mean fool.)

"You still don't believe me," she said into the gaping silence that followed my remark.

"I'm a detective who trusts facts and evidence, not hocus-pocus."

"And yet, here you are with me riding to the scene of the first murder and hoping I can give you a lead to the killer."

I gripped the steering wheel harder and wrung the leather covering in a kind of physical cognitive dissonance against her paranormal nonsense. While the Risperdal kept me from acting out with all sorts of bizarre behavior, the drug didn't interfere with my mind's insistence on orderliness and proof to solve these murders, and my brain couldn't wrap itself around Khoury's equally insistent explanation of astral travel as the answer to the killings.

Even so, after three days of fruitless searching, I had no clues to point me toward any logical reality. Meanwhile, Khoury and Auntie Toy seemed to have an idea who was killing gangbangers. And despite Khoury thinking far past the continuum and her lies about her brother, I had to admit, in the dark recesses of my mind, where logic slept and fantasy prevailed, grew a kernel of hope that she was on to something.

I looked in the rearview mirror. The tan Volvo followed us a few cars back in traffic. And just like that, the real world reasserted itself — Khoury had been playing me.

"Maybe I'm hoping for a lot more," I said, easing my death grip on the wheel.

Hing Hay Park was on our left. I put the blue and white strobe light on the car roof and pulled over. The police tape still wrapped around the pavilion, keeping people out, though a few tourists had gathered, taking pictures.

The tan Volvo drove past. A woman sat at the wheel. Wrong car. Maybe I should have been chastened at my leapt-to conclusion that Khoury was somehow involved. But she gave off the vibe of a woman hiding something. Okay, so vibes were part of the astral bullshit she peddled. Still, my gut was never wrong. Something didn't add up with Madam Khoury, and that made her a suspect for the triad killings. Possibly, she was one of those criminals who inserted themselves into a police investigation for the thrill of being close to the detectives looking for the murderer.

36

Hing Hay Park

During the height of the Han Dynasty, Chinese astronomers divided the sky into four regions represented by mystical creatures: Black Tortoise of the North, White Tiger of the West, Vermilion Bird of the South, and Azure Dragon of the East. Each creature represented a direction and a season, and each had its own characteristics, virtues, and origins. Known as the Four Symbols, the creatures have been used many times in many different aspects of Chinese culture.

The Grand Pavilion in Hing Hay Park is oriented so the four columns holding up the roof line up with the cardinal directions, with bas-relief carvings of the four mystical creatures on their respective pillars. The artists did a fantastic job, and the creatures appear to be waiting for someone to touch them and awaken their esoteric powers. In his last moments, Willie Fong seemed to think so, and as a warlock, he presumably would know. Not that it did him any good. His witchcraft powers might have protected him against rival triads, but not his killer.

· · ·

The walk to the pavilion was slow and silent. Khoury, using whatever paranormal powers she claimed to possess, concentrated on the EMF detector, trying to divine its astral information. I concentrated on her with the observational deductive powers I did possess, waiting for her to slip up.

We crossed under the police tape and entered a scene that to all appearances was anything but a crime. Someone had raked the sand clear of Fong's terrified dash across its grainy contours, and, of course, there had been no blood. The chalk outline of his body had long since disappeared.

But I remembered exactly where we found him, crumpled in an unrecognizable heap of broken bones and a caved-in skull midway between the south and west pillars. The Vermillion Bird — symbolizing rebirth and good fortune — perched on the south column, her scarlet plumage brilliantly colored, head tilted, and beak open as if preening her feathers. On the western column clung the Azure Dragon — symbol of protection. Its head was swiveled to the side, jutting into the pavilion. Rows of gleaming teeth in its hinged jaws appeared ready to snap at the unwary.

Khoury went right to the spot. The EMF detector's case dwarfed her small hands. The loop antenna hummed, and the meter lifted about ten degrees off zero.

"What's that thing going to do?" I asked.

She grimaced but managed to answer civilly. "I told you. It will measure the killer's EMF wavelength."

"Sure, the EMF part I can get, but the antennas... They could be part of a theremin."

She shot a quizzical look at me.

"A device used to make eerie music in twentieth-century sci-fi movies like *The Day the Earth Stood Still*." In addition to film noir, I'm a sci-fi fan. I watched the classics repeatedly growing up.... I really did.

"The theremin part of this device, as you put it, allows my mind to synchronize with Earth's geomagnetic field so I can see who's using it."

"You made this yourself?"

"Yes. Now I need you to be quiet so I can concentrate."

Khoury knelt with the EMF detector in both hands. It emitted a whine straight out of ITV's detective drama, *Midsomer Murders*. The black arrow hand on the green-lit dial moved back and forth in sync with the volume. My brain told me the device was fake. Then again, my flesh crawled, and the hair on the back of my neck stood straight up. I didn't know what to expect. Maybe the boogieman, or ghosts flying out of the rafters, or zombies clawing out of the ground.

Khoury's dark eyes became vacant as the whine increased. Her knuckles whitened on the red chassis. The way she gripped the device, I would have sworn she struggled to keep it from flying out of her hands.

Tourists standing at the edge of the police tape stopped taking pictures and backed away from the pavilion. I stood my ground, though I couldn't help but think they were the sane ones.

The whine grew in pitch and intensity. People covered their ears and ran for the edge of the park. I winced at the noise, which by now had reached the level where, in a few more seconds, I would have to yank the detector from her hands before my eardrums burst.

Khoury gasped and dropped it onto the stone floor. The sound vanished instantly. Sparks shot out of the loop antenna into the Azure Dragon. A low growl filled the quiet, and its iridescent wings appeared to vane up and down. I felt certain the beast was going to climb out of its stony prison and take flight. My hand went to my Glock, as if it would do any good.

The growl became a throaty rasp, and I realized Khoury was making the noise. She fell on her side and rolled over onto her back. Saliva pooled at the corners of her mouth, and she stared into the pavilion's ornate copper ceiling at nothing.

I'm no expert on the occult, but I would have sworn she wasn't faking anything. I grabbed my phone to call the paramedics, when she gasped and rocked to a sitting position. I knelt beside her.

"Get me out of here," she rasped.

I helped her stand and led her toward the street across the sand garden.

"My detector," she said, whirling toward the pavilion.

"No way," I hissed, gripping her elbow tighter. Sure, I didn't believe in paranormal shit, but the inhuman sound issuing from her throat had shaken me to my testicles. "I'm getting us out of here."

She tried to wrench free, and I held her. "I need it," she insisted, jamming in her heels and leaving furrows in the raked sand as I dragged her a couple more steps.

I stopped and faced her. She possessed a fire and strength that at another time and place I would have admired. Right now, I felt an urge to get out of here. Maybe Auntie Toy's not-so-veiled threat that the ghost killer would find me had spooked me. I took a deep breath and convinced myself I was giving in to Khoury's demand because I didn't want a MeToo complaint on my record. "All right, but you stay here. I'll get it."

The EMF's antennas were bent from hitting the floor when she dropped it before keeling over. The glowing dial's needle pulsed as if monitoring a spectral heartbeat. It hummed against the stones, and I half expected it to spin in my hands if I picked it up. But as soon as I touched the vibrating red case, the needle pegged zero, and the device went silent. Guess I didn't have the mojo to operate it. Still, an electric shiver coursed up my spine, and I carried the detector gingerly with two fingers to where Khoury waited.

She hugged it to her until we were in the car.

"What happened back there?" I asked. "And don't tell me you saw a ghost."

"Not here," she said, looking at the pavilion as if it harbored a homicidal maniac.

She was adamant, so I said, "I know a coffee house on Capitol Hill... the Hidden Corner."

37

Capitol Hill
The Hidden Corner

C hinatown has all the varied flavors of Asia, from the Bay of Bengal
to the Sea of Japan, packed into a small area. The different ethnic
groups live in reasonable peace together, mostly because the Police Tong
insists on it.

The cultures of the Middle East, on the other hand, are spread around
Seattle as if they can't stand to be near one another. A Persian restaurant
beside the Seattle Center; a Greek restaurant in the U District; falafels in
Northgate; a Turkish coffeehouse at the Pike Street Market. You get the
picture.

It just so happens the best Lebanese food is on Capitol Hill, the Hidden
Corner, owned by a man whose name is unpronounceable. I speak Arabic,
and I can't pronounce it. Everyone calls him Pop.

The Hidden Corner occupies a small building on Mercer and Broadway. From the outside, the tiny shop looks smaller than a hole in the wall.
Inside is a bazaar of spices and coffee mixed with the tantalizing aromas of
lamb, beef, grilled chicken, deep-fried chickpeas, and tahini. On a warm
day with the windows and doors open, the restaurant's buffet of tanta-

lizing odors drifts into the street and has been known to cause fender-benders.

The Hidden Corner's parking lot had enough room for ten compact cars or four SUVs and half a dozen Vespas. It was full, and the street offered no open spots anywhere near the place. Apparently, the threat of a war in the Asian community didn't bother Middle Easterners at all, and they went happily about their business.

We finally found a car pulling out of a space a couple of blocks away. I started to pull in when a guy in front honked and brandished a fist at me. He got out of his car. I flashed my badge. He flashed me the finger but moved on.

I had never been in the Hidden Corner with a Lebanese woman before — we're talking an unmarried, unveiled woman. The restaurant is also a hookah lounge. Several Middle Eastern men sat cross-legged at round low tables eating finger foods and smoking. They were mostly Lebanese and Syrian ex-pats. By the looks Khoury and I got walking through the door, some of these guys had never heard of the twentieth century, let alone the twenty-first.

The heavy smell of hashish hung in the air. I didn't do anything because Washington State's recreational marijuana laws defined marijuana as any part of the cannabis plant, including hashish and hashish oil. I insisted on a seat near the French doors leading onto a patio, where the odor of cannabis wasn't as strong and wouldn't bother me.

As a beat cop, I had visited the Hidden Corner a lot because I loved the dolma, moussaka, and homemade pita bread. (As good as Mama's naan, though I'd never tell her that.) But it had been a long time since I last visited here. I didn't even know if Pop would remember me.

He came over immediately. Pop was as old as Methuselah, with a gray beard, gray hair, and gray bushy eyebrows to match. The lines in his cheeks had deepened since I last saw him, but the perpetual smile welcomed us. He remembered enough to call me Jack. I asked him how his wife was doing, and he answered, "Still cooking. As long as she lives, this place will stay open." He took our orders for coffee (Pop has a Palestinian friend who sells him the best Arabica coffee beans in the world come from his small farm in Ethiopia) and an appetizer tray of baba ghanouj, hummus, dolma, and pita bread.

Our food and the coffee came within minutes. Maybe Pop sensed we needed privacy, because when a table opened up next to us, he refused let anyone sit there.

I sipped the strong brew, made with a touch of sheep milk and a hint of unrefined sugar, the way it had been made in Yemen 600 years ago. "So the legend goes," Pop said. I believed him.

Setting the delicate demitasse down next to the small coffee urn, I said, "Give, and I'd better not think you're faking any of it." After the scare at the pavilion, coffee and food were all the charity I was willing to extend to Khoury at present.

She paused and downed the coffee like a slug of whiskey to calm her nerves. I'll say this for Khoury: she might have been some half-baked psychic, but she was as smart as her PhD indicated. She laid it out in easy-to-understand sentences.

"Dynamo theory describes the process through which a rotating, convecting, and electrically conducting fluid can maintain a magnetic field. A dynamo is thought to be the source of the Earth's magnetic field."

"What does that have to do with your astral plane hocus-pocus?"

"The astral plane connects to Earth's magnetic field because it shares the same frequency. It's called the Schumann resonance. I built the EMF detector. Whoever holds it can get in tune with the field, if they have the proper training and the strength of mind to focus their thoughts on the frequency."

"Like a Wi-Fi hot spot," I said, this time without any attitude.

"The astral plane is a nonphysical realm of existence where various psychic and paranormal phenomena are possible and where every human body has a unique non-physical counterpart."

"Even me," I said, the words sounding less whimsical aloud than they had in my head.

"Even you." She smiled, then came the kicker: "I've been training with the device for three years now. Whoever is committing these murders is out for revenge. The men he's killed caused the death of loved ones."

"What loved ones?"

"It was hard to see clearly through the rage, but as near as I can tell, it was a family."

Shades of Auntie Toy. Andrew Chapman flashed in my mind once more — a dead end, literally and figuratively. No way he had enough working gray matter left to go anywhere on the astral plane or any other plane. It was a shame really. I had done some digging into Chapman's past, and he would have been the foremost suspect of Dr. Khoury's astral plane murders because of his research into the same shit she investigated.

In fact, he wrote the book on it, proving what Khoury had just explained — astral travel was possible if a person could tune his brain's electro-magnetic frequency to the frequency of the Earth. Capitalizing on his notoriety, Chapman had become an overnight sensation and multimillionaire, with a weekly podcast. Now his cousins wanted his money.

Fuck his cousins. They're bastards.

"Is something wrong?" Khoury asked.

She must have seen me grimace, or maybe it was my eyes. They weren't darting everywhere. They focused on the fork in my hand, which I held with the intensity of jabbing it into somebody's ear. It was during these moments when I was most grateful for the Risperdal. Without it, I would have seriously considered taking the cousins to some remote clearing in the Cascades and wasting them, because they were asshole vermin who didn't deserve the label *human beings* and should be put down.

"Nothing," I said. "I was thinking about a guy I know. Your EMF crystal ball tell you who we're looking for?"

She shook her head. "I've got his signature but not enough residual energy to trace him. Still..." She fell silent, not as with a normal pause in conversation, but as if she were perplexed, even a little scared.

"Still what?" I pressed.

"I get the feeling this man was somehow familiar. I..." She shook her head. "I'm sorry. The EMF... It can only measure the killer's electromagnetic signature. It can't actually identify him."

Maybe the cousins still chapped my ass, and I said with a little more heat than I intended, "And maybe you're leaving out the part that the killer's the guy following you in the tan Volvo — your brother, Mahir."

That got her attention. She took a sip of coffee, ate some of the hummus with pita, wiped her mouth daintily with a napkin, and said softly, "Mahir is a misguided young man."

"Tell me about him. What's his connection to the killings?"

"Mahir is not the killer."

"Why is he following you?"

"It's a family matter."

"What kind of family matter?"

For the first time, I got under her cool veneer to the outside world, and she answered with her own heat, "A private one. I can handle it."

"I don't disagree you can handle yourself, but you inserted yourself into a police investigation then lied to me about your brother following you. Not exactly the way to gain my trust."

"Everything I've told you about these killings is true. How can I convince you?"

"Tell me what's going on with your brother."

She lowered her gaze. "It would bring shame upon my parents."

Maybe Mahir Khoury screwed goats. And no, I didn't say that aloud. Some lines even I won't cross.

We were at an impasse. The thing with her brother inclined me not to trust her, in spite of the science surrounding her EMF findings.

(Yeah, and maybe you're thinking, *Look, dimwad, she knows the signature. Why not drive around the city until you pick up his scent?* Because, dimwad, Seattle's huge, and millions of people live here and in the surrounding areas. Besides, if the killer really was using the astral plane, he could be flying in from Monkey's Eyebrow, Kentucky.)

We finished the meal in silence. The other men in the place continued to stare at us. They spoke in Arabic, making lewd comments about the type of unmarried woman Khoury must be to sit in public with a man. She blushed several times.

Me? ...My face flushed, and my eyes darted wildly from side to side. I wanted to smash the grinning mouths and stuff the snide laughter down some throats to cool my already jangly nerves. And I might have — the Risperdal only goes so far; the rest of my control is by will alone — but a surprise passed by outside the coffeehouse that drained away all my rage at these sneering fools. My mother strolled by arm in arm with a strange man, looking as if she hadn't a care in the world.

38

Café Wrangler

C apitol Hill is packed with hip bars, bistros, gay clubs, indie shops, Volunteer Park, and Lake View Cemetery, where the city's founders and Bruce Lee are buried. Fifty years later, people still leave flowers on Lee's grave, but no one visits the city's founders, though Denny Park and a street, Denny Way, are named after them. It seems altogether fitting and proper that a Chinese American film star would be the most revered icon in a city that denigrated its Chinese citizens at every turn in the late 1800s.

Mama was supposed to be home taking care of Pops.

I bolted to my feet, kicking the chair back so hard it tipped over, hitting the floor with a crash like dishes breaking. The hustle and bustle of conversation in the Hidden Corner went silent. Pop's bushy eyebrows arched at the sharp intrusion into the coffeehouse's normally affable atmosphere. I shook my head at him apologetically and concentrated on the pair walking away.

Pulling a hundred from Willie Chen's roll, I slammed it on the table to pay for the meal and a Lyft for Khoury. "I'm sorry, but you'll have to find your way back to the precinct on your own. I have an errand to run."

Khoury touched my sleeve. "Things are not what they appear," she said kindly.

I got the sense she wasn't talking about her brother or the triad murders and answered in my best glib Irish voice, "They never are."

I followed my mother and her date to Café Wrangler about a block and a half from the Hidden Corner. The two places couldn't be more different. The Wrangler is so upscale, if you aren't a rich snob, you won't get a table. The restaurant provides exotic meats — legal and in season — from around the globe. The prices match the upper crust, high-end, chi-chi taste of the décor. They're so far above my pay grade that I can't even afford to go into the place and look at the menu.

So why was Mama eating at this swank place?

Café Wrangler had outdoor seating. Mama and her date sat together, holding hands as if they had nothing to hide. One of Capitol Hill's numerous food trucks had set up in a parking lot across the street. It advertised new age, wholesome, good-for-you, hippie food from two generations ago. I ordered the ultra-healthy, all-veggie, non-GMO, locally grown kale smoothie, managed a sip without puking, and sat at the makeshift patio with folding chairs and tables the owner set up around his mobile place of business. I had a good view of my mom and *the guy*. I hoped she wasn't footing the bill. It would set her and my dad's social security income back months.

Watching them, the old joke about walking in on your parents when they're kissing came to mind. I had a front row seat to woo and coo. The guy gave Mom a peck on the cheek, and she leaned into it. Gag me with a Smurf. My eyes darted everywhere but at them.

I had to do something to settle my urge to punch the guy with my Glock before shooting him, so I took a picture of the bozo. Okay, he didn't have a red nose, green wig, and floppy shoes. He dressed conservatively in a nice suit and broad blue tie with a Windsor knot.

But from the way he held Mama's hand while pushing a strand of hair back from her cheek, I knew the two of them were doing a lot more than taking long heart-to-heart walks together.

At any rate, I used a facial recognition app on my phone to find out who the schmoozer was. Since I'm a cop, the app connected directly to the database used by Seattle Police Department's street cams to identify perps. I provided my badge number and a reason for the search — I said, "Chinatown murders" — and the answer came back in minutes instead of hours or even days.

My mom's date was Clive Henderson, the owner of a computer-engineering firm that had contracts with Google, Apple, and Microsoft. In short, he put the L in loaded. So, he wasn't a serial murderer or con man. But, hell, he leaned across the table and kissed my mom, a married woman, and she shouldn't have been out with this guy in the first place.

I wondered if Mama were playing him in order to get money to pay for dad's health care. But the way she leaned into old Clive's kiss — according to his bio, he was ten years older than her, but he hid his age as well as she did — told me this date wasn't harmless gold-digging.

I looked away and called home. Luis was still on the job. I could hear Spanish obscenities in the background. Guess Pops hadn't won a game yet. Luis told me Mom hadn't come home. I didn't tell him I was looking at her, but I did make up my mind what to do. I said, "She'll be there shortly. Can you hang on for a while longer, Luis?"

He said sure.

I hung up and called the precinct to request personal time. McCrory didn't snicker. Liam always knew when something had me bent out of shape. "Your mom again?"

"Yeah."

"You need help finding her?"

'No... I'm looking at her and her date."

"Date?" he repeated then added, "You need back up?"

"I can handle this *gadè* by myself," I said.

"For him, not you."

"I'm calm," I insisted.

"Yeah, right. You start swearing in Punjabi, Jack, and I get worried. Promise you'll be nice."

I ended the call with Liam swearing at me in Gaelic.

The waiter brought drinks to the happy couple. Better now than when the main course arrived. With Liam's advice rumbling in the back of my head, I slowly walked up to them. With no idea of a witty way to break into a hot date between my mom and somebody other than my dad, I said, "Hi, Mama," and flashed my badge at Clive. He sat very still. *Good boy. McCrory won't have to worry about me.*

I said, "C'mon, Mama. We're going home. Pops needs you."

The genuine surprise on Clive's face told me she hadn't mentioned anything about her married life. She started to object, but when disappointment replaced bewilderment on old Clive, she came along meekly.

On the way home, I called Dr. Herschel. I asked him to stop by now instead of waiting until this evening. After hearing why, he agreed to meet us.

I had all sorts of questions, but the way mom sat in the passenger seat, as if she hadn't a care in the world and hadn't done anything wrong, told me I wouldn't get the answer to the most important one: What did you do to Mama? That would be up to Dr. Herschel.

39

Ravenna

The Ravenna neighborhood takes its name from a nearby creek, which flows through a ravine, dropping 115 feet from Ravenna Park at the top to Cowen Park at the bottom. It's a beautiful green space with lots of running trails; it's also spooky, especially during the gloaming, as my Irish ancestors described twilight's witching hours. As a kid, I often played beside the fast-running stream and among the towering trees until long-fingered eldritch shadows stretched across the darkening paths, and with fearsome tales of banshees and púcas dancing in my not-so-level head, I bolted up the main trail out of the gloom like ghosts were chasing me.

Ravenna isn't quite as terrifying — a middle-income, working-class neighborhood. Residents know the families living ten houses down as well as the couple living next door. These are the people who bring gifts to your daughter's wedding, shout congratulations after your son scores the winning touchdown, and who will attend your funeral. Most of them go to the same doctor. In this case, Dr. Herschel. All of them eventually know your business.

· · ·

When the neighbors on either side of my parents' place and across the street saw me drive up with my mom and Dr. Herschel arrive moments later, they knew something was amiss. They probably thought it had to do with my dad, unless they saw how my mom was dressed as if coming home from a night out with a lover.

I herded my mom inside. She waved at all of them. They waved back and shouted hello at Dr. Herschel. He waved but didn't say anything and entered the home with Mama and me as though it were the most normal of things to do on a late weekday morning.

Pops sat in his wheelchair in the back room looking out at the yard. Luis was in the kitchen getting him some orange juice.

"Luis," I said, "thanks for staying extra. I've got it from here."

"No problem, Mr. Doyle," he answered with a genuine smile. "Your dad is a terrific old man."

I saw him to the door and shoved another hundred from Chen's roll at him. Then I checked on Pops, giving him the orange juice. I tucked the blanket around him. Even in the warmth of August, he was chilly most days.

"Your mom finally home?" he asked.

"Yes. She's in the kitchen with Dr. Herschel." A frown creased his weathered face, and I hastily added, "Everything's fine. Just a routine checkup. You know Mama. She won't go to the doctor, so I brought him to her. He'll check in on you later."

Pops grunted. I sat down next to him, and we watched squirrels play tag through the trees.

I checked in with McCrory; after all, I still had several Chinatown murders to solve, and Uncle Lo's deadline wasn't getting any longer. Liam swore at me in Gaelic — man, he can cuss louder and with more variety than a shipload of sailors. When he paused for a breath, I asked him if Malvern had asked for me yet.

"The boss has been on the phone with the mayor for fifteen minutes. That's a personal record. You'd better get your ass back here ASAP."

"I will, but I'm home, and Dr. Herschel is examining Mama."

That was enough to quiet Liam's tongue, and he signed off with a short, "Call if you need anything."

Twenty minutes later, Dr. Herschel came into the room. He asked dad how he was doing and did a cursory examination. He finally stood up, pulled on his long earlobes, and announced, "You'll outlive us all, Henry."

Pops snorted. "As far as you're concerned. Hell, I don't mind if I go first. It's those other bastards whose graves I want to dance on."

Dr. Herschel patted him on the shoulder. "I'll do the best I can to see you live to do that, Henry."

Doc crooked a finger at me, and I followed him out of the house to his car, a Volvo sedan older than me that he kept tuned himself. Therapy, he called it.

He leaned against the side, wiped his brow with an old bandana, and got right to the point with an obscure question. "Your mom's maiden name?"

"Bhatt. Her mother's husband had been a chemist in Pakistan before Partition. Why you ask, doc?"

"Just now, when I asked her name, she answered Bhatt, not Doyle. When I asked what she'd been up to the last few weeks, she winked at me and told me in great detail all the men she'd been seeing. When I asked about Henry's health, she rolled her eyes and said he was fine and didn't care what she did." Dr. Herschel's eyebrows arched with the universal doctor expression — *any of that sound right to you?*

I shook my head, helplessly drawn to clichés as a way of fighting against what Dr. Herschel implied. "What's it all mean, doc?"

He bit his lower lip. "There's no way to sugar coat this, Jack. Your mom is displaying classic symptoms of FTD."

I knew he wasn't talking about floral arrangements. "Some kind of tumor? Cancer?"

He shook his head and spoke with a soft, somber hopelessness. "Frontotemporal dementia. It's an umbrella term for a group of brain disorders that primarily affect the frontal and temporal lobes of the brain... the areas generally associated with personality, behavior, and language. In FTD, these lobes shrink, and depending on which part of the brain is affected most, people display dramatic changes in personality. Some become socially inappropriate, impulsive, or emotionally indifferent. Some lose the ability to use language properly."

His tone told me there was no cure. I sagged against his car as if a mule had kicked me.

He went on even more softly and somberly, which didn't make the moment any easier to take. "Of course, I need to do an MRI to confirm what I suspect, but..." He shrugged the shrug of a doctor who knows his diagnosis is correct and doesn't need a fancy machine to tell him so. "She'll need round-the-clock care either at a facility or here at home."

"Sounds expensive," I said, trying to wrap my head around what he was saying.

"Indeed, Medicare doesn't cover of frontotemporal dementia."

"What can I do?" I asked, completely out of my depth and with no friggin' clue how to proceed. The care he mentioned would cost a lot more than my parents had in savings. Without Medicare, they'd be bankrupt in a year. Willie Chen's $10,000 would buy a few months. I thought about the Police Brotherhood's Cayman accounts, but they were off limits. Others in the brotherhood had faced family medical emergencies, and no one had dipped into the funds. And asking Pamela for help wasn't a road I could go down comfortably. Maybe a week ago, before Cassandra showed up in my life again. But since then, a glacier had been growing between us, and it didn't take a rocket scientist or a marriage counselor to see where our relationship was headed.

Dr. Herschel saw my helplessness and stepped up. He's a mensch. "I suggest you contact the young man I met when I walked in and see if he can stay here for the next few nights to help take care of your parents while you set things up for something more permanent. Perhaps relatives can help."

Other relatives didn't exist. My mom was an only child, and my dad's brother had died years ago with no children. Luis would have to do for now.

Dr. Herschel stared into my face. His eyes followed my rapid eye movements. "How's the TD?"

I pulled it together. "Manageable."

"The Risperdal taking care of the other stuff?"

"So far." I was out of pills. It would be two or three days before I showed any symptoms. I had time to refill the prescription.

"Good. Look, I'm always available. I'll make some calls and see if I can't find some home health care company that can give you a break on fees."

He got into his Volvo and drove off. Mama waved from the front door.

My phone pinged. It was Liam with a text, warning me Malvern had finished his talk with the mayor and wanted me in the squad room, sooner rather than later.

I texted back requesting personal time for family matters and sketched out the details. Okay, maybe I didn't elaborate, since it took me two seconds to reply, *He can kiss my ass.*

Be serious, Jack, Liam cautioned.

I did a counting exercise — backwards from 100 to zero by sevens — Dr. Herschel taught me when I was a teenager to help control my impulses. A minute later, I asked Liam to explain to Malvern that I was taking a personal day.

"Your mom going to be all right, Jack?" he asked.

"I don't know, Liam. I'll call you later when I've had a chance to collect myself."

I put my phone away and stared at the house without really seeing it, just the people inside. My parents were all at once old and frail — the two people I could always count on to save me, and there was nothing I could do to help them. It was moments like these I cursed the Risperdal for taking me out of my own tiny world, with its mirrored walls and ceiling and floor reflecting the only thing in the world that mattered.

Flinging those thoughts aside, I gathered myself and went inside.

I didn't respond to texts or calls the rest of the day, figuring Liam would cover for me. I took care of family as well as I could. Luis said he'd to come back in the evening and stay through the night in case Pops needed help. He also said he'd check with coworkers to see if anyone would take extra shifts until we found a permanent home health care company. Mama agreed to stay home at least for the next couple of days, though she didn't think her going out was a big deal.

In the evening before I went home, I called Liam and told him what was going on. "Whatever you need," he answered, like the true friend he was. Then I called Malvern and told him I had personal matters with my parents but didn't elaborate. It stifled his wrath for now. But if another triad died, I'd find myself in the deep end of the shit pool.

40

Madison Park

I once asked Mama what it was like growing up in a Punjabi family in the US. She said, "Like any family, there were good times and bad times." When I asked what they did during the bad times, she answered with great solemnity, "We ate. After a good meal, everything is better, and you can forgive anyone, even family." Maybe that's why I've never heard her and Pops say a bad word to each other.

Pamela didn't share my mother's convictions. Dinner was a chilly, silent affair, and by the end, I was exhausted from dodging my girlfriend's stony glares and Hagler's angry stares.

By the way Pamela shifted her attention from Hagler to me, it was obvious she resented Cassandra, and Hagler's presence only increased her rage. His scowls, on the other hand, convinced me he had spoken with his wife and knew for certain I was going to accompany her to the abortion clinic. Dinner ended, thankfully, with the only further injuries being emotional scarring.

"I have an early morning," Pamela said in her pointed manner, which meant, *Don't disturb me, ass face.* Okay, maybe I'm reading some of my own anger in her mood, but she hadn't smiled, let alone hugged or kissed me, since I got home. Plus, she took the wine bottle from the table with her. Pamela's anything but a lush. She drinks wine at the dinner table because it's chic, not because she has to have it.

Hagler waved at me, and I followed him into the den. He closed the door behind me, and when I turned, he lashed out with his fist, clipping me on the chin. I staggered backward. "You son of a bitch," he yelled. "You're taking Cassie to get an abortion." He launched a wild haymaker at my head. I ducked under it, and he spun awkwardly into the couch, banging his shoulder against the armrest. His glasses flew off and skittered across the parquet flooring toward the fireplace.

He pushed himself up, swinging at the same time.

I jabbed him with a right in the stomach, and he folded into the cushions, gasping for breath. "Stay down," I warned. I went over to the bar and poured a brandy. "You're right," I said, handing the beveled glass to him. "I should have told you when you first asked. And you're right to hate me for betraying you."

He started crying. I waited him out, figuring Hagler knew he'd married way above his pay grade, and all the anger and bluster had surfaced because he feared losing the one thing that made him feel good about himself.

If you're wondering why I was so certain about Hagler's emotions, it's because I had felt the same way with Cassandra. She had this way of making me think I was the only person in the world who mattered.

He stopped sobbing long enough for me to encourage him to drink. He drained it, and I poured him another while he picked up his glasses. Sitting in the chair across from him, I waited again, sipping the Irish whiskey Pamela kept here for me and thinking about what a jerk I was for agreeing to Cassandra's request. Sure, I was still in love with her, but the last thing I wanted was to wreck

Hagler's marriage. Okay, maybe that wasn't the last thing I wanted, but I wasn't some shameless man-slut who would hurt others to get his way.

(BTW, I'm only insightful about myself when I've had a couple of whiskeys. The rest of the time, not even the great anti-hero Sam Spade could keep up with the twists and turns of my self-absorbed mind.)

Finally, Hagler looked up from his brandy glass. He wiped his eyes with the back of his hand. "What am I going to do, Jack? I can't lose her. I'd be lost without her. She's the best thing that ever happened to me."

(Yeah, people really do talk in clichés like soap opera characters. It's because they best express the trials, tribulations, and hurts we experience on a daily basis in a way others can relate to.)

I fired back at him. "Listen to her, *gūgā cūrā*."

He looked at me blankly.

"It's a Punjabi word that roughly translates to 'manure for brains.'"

"I'm a dumbshit, huh."

"You got it."

(Mama mostly yelled it at drivers, but also anyone who didn't move quickly enough for her. She got the same blank looks as I did. On the other hand, it absolutely kills in Chandigarh.)

I took a sip of whiskey. "Try to see things her way. Cassandra needs your help not your disapproval. It's important to her that you support her decision, because her parents won't. Hell, they'll disown her for even thinking about an abortion let alone getting one."

The anguish on Hagler's face was easy to read. He was a devout Catholic. He even read the Bible in Latin. It would be easier for him to gnaw off his own arm than go against holy Church doctrine on abortion. At the same time, those clichés he'd spouted about Cassandra were more powerful. He really would die if he lost her.

"You know what you have to do, Mel," I said softly.

He brooded into his brandy for a minute before raising his glass toward mine. "I will," he promised. We clinked and drank, sealing the deal. We refrained from throwing the glasses into the fireplace. It held gas logs and didn't carry the cachet of a real roaring fire.

I finished my drink and got up to leave. Hagler waved me back down. "What about your problem?" he said.

I started to deny anything was wrong, and he stood, took the glass from my hand, and refilled it and his, both with whiskey this time. He handed it to me and sat back down. "You haven't said two words about your day since you picked me up at the ME's office. And I happen to know you spent the entire time at your parents. Liam told me," he added before I could object.

He was right. I needed to tell someone, and Hagler was a doctor — an ME, but still a doctor. I laid out what was happening with my mom. He listened without cracking a smile, which I thought showed good manners as well as support.

He set his glass on the arm of the couch, steepled his fingers, and said, "Sounds like frontotemporal dementia."

"Dr. Herschel said the same."

Hagler shook his head forlornly and said, "I'm sorry, Jack. I'm sure Herschel told you there's no cure."

I nodded.

"You'll have to find caregivers. Soon, too, I imagine. While it may seem as if she can take care of herself now, if the disease progresses rapidly, she'll become a danger to herself as well as others around her."

Dr. Herschel hadn't been this blunt. On the other hand, as a detective, I could read between the lines, which had been the cause for my silence Hagler picked up on during the ride home.

You know those awkward moments truth creates during a conversation, where to continue speaking is to risk repeating yourself until everyone is tired and forgets what was originally said. Hagler and I had reached the point of inane repetition.

Luckily, Pamela yelled at me from the top of the stairs to come to bed.

Hagler saluted me with his empty glass. "Thanks," he said. "I'm going to call Cassandra right now." He shook a finger at me and grinned.

I couldn't have been more unsettled by his smile if he'd sported long, gleaming vampire canines. "What?" I asked warily.

"You'd better wear some knee pads. After the dirty looks she threw you at dinner tonight, you've got some serious begging to do, my friend."

PART IV

AN UNDISCOVERED COUNTRY

41

Greenbrier Nursing Home

Geneva Bowen strode through the Greenbrier Nursing Home's double doors with vengeful purpose. Five of the I-5 Dragon gangbangers were dead, and according to her detective brother, the triad was reeling from the killings, its operations in Seattle torn apart. *Soon... Soon, they'll be completely destroyed*, she exulted.

The thought of another night exterminating those animals exhilarated her and fed her resolve to a single-mindedness that shut out everything else. So great was her determination, she almost breezed past the reception desk without chatting up Clara.

She slowed her pace and stopped, surprised to find Myrna Toy sitting behind the glass enclosure. Geneva glanced at her watch — just after 10:00 pm. "You're here early tonight, Myrna."

The young nurse looked up from her computer screen. "Clara wasn't feeling well, and I offered to fill." She bit her lower lip. "It seems to be going around. The security guard left with a bad headache an hour ago."

Geneva glanced at the empty desk where the young college

student, Murray, usually sat, head buried in a schoolbook. "Don't worry," she said in her most soothing ER nurse voice. "Nothing bad will happen. We're a nursing home, not a 7-Eleven."

Myrna smiled gratefully. "I checked in on Mr. Chapman earlier tonight. He's going to need a bath and a shave tomorrow."

"That won't be necessary." Geneva held up a compact blue DOPP kit with the Harborview Medical Center logo on the side. "I'll do it while I'm here tonight."

Myrna's smile widened. "Thanks, Ms. Bowen. I'm sure Mr. Chapman appreciates all you do for him. I certainly do." She touched a button on the computer screen, and a section darkened. "There, I've turned off the camera in Mr. Chapman's room to give you privacy."

"Thank you," Geneva said.

Impatient to get on with God's business of wiping out the Dragons, she hurried down the hall, past open doors of dying, deserted patients grateful no other visitors were here this evening, yet strangely scornful of their absence from the bedside of their loved ones. She didn't notice Myrna thoughtfully watching her or the young Chinese American touch the computer screen a second time. The camera in Chapman's room flickered back to life.

Geneva wrung out the washcloth, steaming from scalding water, until it was warm and damp. She didn't mind the heat. She ran it softly over Andrew Chapman's arms and hands, careful not to disturb the IV giving him fluids or the feeding tube providing nourishment. She bathed his legs and torso, then wrapped the warm cloth around his cheeks and chin before retrieving a straight razor and shaving gel from the DOPP kit. Removing the cloth, she lathered his cheeks and throat and deftly shaved his two-day-old beard. She wiped off the excess soap and combed his hair. Next, she did his nails.

"Five of the Dragons are dead, thanks to you, Andrew," she said conversationally, as though talking with an old friend.

Chapman's eyelids twitched as if in REM sleep.

"Most of the leadership is gone and the ones who are left are scared. Soon, the Dragons will be nothing more than a list of dead gangbangers in police files." She gripped both his hands in hers, as if holding them in prayer. "Then you can join your family."

The EEG machine clicked softly, and its tinted green screen marked subtle changes in Chapman's brain waves before subsiding once more to a flat line.

Geneva allowed herself a grim smile. "And your two girls and my niece's death at the hands of those animals will be avenged at last." She frowned. *Animals is too good a word for them. Monsters, beasts, unholy savages is what they are.*

A soft rustle of clothes and hurried tiptoeing away from the door interrupted Geneva's angry thoughts. She put Chapman's hands gently on the sheets and patted him on the arm. "I'll be right back. Some very rude person eavesdropped on our private conversation."

In the hall, she could hear footsteps scurrying toward the night duty nurse's station. Geneva sidled after the culprit, staying in the shadows so she wouldn't be seen. Stopping at the end of the hall, she peered around the corner and saw Myrna calling someone on her cell phone.

"Auntie Toy... it's Myrna... Yes, your grandniece. Yes, I'm fine, but I have something to tell you. It's very important. Something very strange is going on here at the nursing home. Mom told me you thought the triad killer was a ghost, and I think maybe you could be right. I think one of the patients might be responsible for the killings."

Geneva bit her lip to keep from gasping aloud. She listened carefully as Myrna told her great aunt about Chapman's fluctuating EEG readings, the strange flickering of the lights on the nights of the murders, and what she had overheard standing outside Andrew Chapman's room.

Geneva pressed against the wall and leaned forward, trying to catch Auntie Toy's response. In the still quiet of the hallway, the old woman's anxious voice was a tinny whisper of indistinguishable sounds. However, the reaction on Myrna's face and her responses were like reading a book to Geneva, an experienced ER nurse who often dealt with patients who could do little more than nod or groan at questions.

"Myrna, listen carefully. You must leave at once."

"Auntie Toy, that's impossible. I have patients. I can't leave them."

"Niece, listen to your Auntie. You aren't safe there. Leave right away. Don't go home. Get out of Seattle someplace where no one knows you. And whatever you do, don't call anyone."

Myrna's stomach twisted at the warning. She knew her great aunt dabbled in the occult, and she felt as if the world of the supernatural was about to break upon her. She slewed her head around and, even though she saw nothing unnatural racing toward her, ducked partly beneath the desk as if making herself a smaller target. "What's going on, Auntie? You're scaring me."

"I'm sorry, child. There's no time to explain, and I can't protect you if you stay. On your life, you must leave, and no matter what you hear on the news, don't come home until Uncle Lo calls and says it's safe. Do this for me. Now!"

The fear in her great aunt's voice galvanized Myrna. "Yes, Auntie." She ended the call, glanced once around the room, picked up her purse, and ran out of the building.

When Myrna ended the call, Geneva hurried back to Chapman's room. She closed the door to make sure they couldn't be overheard by any of the other staff. Leaning over his still form, she whispered, "The young night duty nurse told Auntie Toy about us. You must stop her before she goes to the police."

Chapman's eyelids flickered briefly then stilled.

Geneva leaned in closer, her voice more insistent. "If you don't stop her, others will be hurt the same as your family. And your husband and beautiful daughters will have died in vain. You must not let anything stand in our way."

The EEG machine rattled in response. The lights dimmed, and the temperature in the room fell until Geneva could see her breath. Chapman's face and hands glowed, and it seemed for a moment as if his body grew larger. Then the aura surrounding his still form drifted slowly upward like a cloud of dense vapor rising from the earth, revealing the pale skeletal figure beneath. The emanation hovered and with equal slowness morphed into Chapman's strong build and handsome features from before the terrible tragedy that destroyed his family and put him in a coma. Yet, the transformation did not stop there. The anguish at the terrible thing Geneva asked him to do, which he knew he must do in order to avenge his family, deepened until his blue eyes became red embers and burned like the fires of the damned.

Geneva stumbled backward toward the open window. Her breath caught in her throat at the fiery figure filling the space above the bed with an ogreish menace. She stood still a moment, frightened she might have pushed Chapman too far in the quest for vengeance. Then she sensed rage become overwhelming reluctance and knew he had reconciled the death of one to protect the many.

Chapman's pulsing ghostly image hovered. Sparking arcs snaked from the EEG, the monitor, light fixtures, and electrical outlets to his body. It seemed to Geneva like he was gathering energy, not only from the machines but from her own essence as well. Every passing second, his aura brightened until it became a dazzling sun.

Rather than shrink away, she stood tall — bathed in the deepening glow, blond hair no longer in tight curls but straight, and her dark skin gleaming like the sun's corona during a solar eclipse — ecstatic to provide him with whatever he needed to be successful.

Transfixed by the beautiful avenging image of Chapman, for several seconds, Geneva could not speak but gazed with loving fondness upon him. When at last she found her voice, the words came from the well of her throat in a deep basso like a requiem. "Stay strong, and you will end the threat of the triads in Seattle forever. Go. Now. Protect our legacy."

The sound of a train rushing past filled the air as Chapman's astral self-hurtled out of the room into Seattle's dark night. In the wake that followed, Geneva collapsed onto her knees and began to pray.

42

Northgate, Seattle
Khoury's Home

I t was almost midnight, and Zaina Khoury sat cross-legged on the thick wool carpet in the living room of her modest two-bedroom bungalow. The electromagnetic field detector hummed softly on the fireplace's blue stone hearth.

For the past hour, conflicting memories of her home in the small village of Zawatar ash Sharqiyat, near the Litani River in Lebanon, had prevented her from visiting the astral plane to find the triad killer. Until her mind settled, she would not be able to undertake her quest. So, she set aside her eager anticipation and allowed her thoughts to meander through her past.

Life in the small town had been idyllic. Khoury's family had not been impacted by the ongoing war with the Israelis, and, as a young girl, she had known peace and happiness. Then she discovered physics, and her dreamy childhood became a nightmare.

At first her family had blocked her attempts to further her education. The idea of a young woman going away to college went against the small village's traditional values. But as the youngest and most favored daughter, she had prevailed against the community's inflexibility, where her older sisters could not, and had attended the American University of Beirut.

Yet, even out of sight, tradition eventually caught up with her. In her first year of graduate studies, her parents insisted she return to the village for an arranged marriage to a much older devout Muslim in his fifties, who would not have allowed a young wife out of the house. Khoury refused the match and continued her studies in Beirut, thinking that would be the last of such nonsense. Her parents disowned her, charging she had brought great shame to the family and denying her any more financial support.

On her own for the first time, Khoury did not surrender her dreams but found work at a women's health care clinic to pay for her studies. Four years later, she graduated first in her class.

Khoury sighed at the memory of what should have been a day of joy and distinction. She had been the first woman in her family to graduate from college and go on to earn a doctorate. The day had been bittersweet. No one from her family had shown up for the ceremony. She was truly dead to them. Disillusionment and disappointment weighed heavily on her, and she had had to bite her lip to keep from crying in shame and unbearable loneliness. Afterwards, the university president shook her hand personally and announced she had been offered a teaching position. The whipsaw of emotions wracked her, but this time she cried tears of joy for a severing of past connections and a portal to a bright future.

Five years later, on track for tenure, her bright prospects abruptly changed with her study of the occult and the relationship between the Earth's magnetic field and the astral plane.

Khoury sighed at the memory. *Every life has its peaks and valleys,* she thought. *Even the Prophet Muhammad was forced to flee his home in Mecca. America is my Hegira... and all because of the EMF detector I invented.*

A year ago, she had found refuge in Seattle, where she received a position as an adjunct physics professor at the small North Seattle College in the neighborhood of Northgate. It allowed her time to work on her passion of bringing mainstream science to the occult. It had also brought her close to one of her heroes, Andrew Chapman, a fellow researcher of the astral plane. Though they shared emails, she had never actually met the man. His untimely accident just weeks after she arrived in the States left her alone and abandoned once again. Fortunately, her faith in physics sustained her. And she had thrown herself into the study of the occult, mastering the EMF detector.

Khoury held her breath and let it out slowly. She added more pieces of white sandalwood to an iron brazier sitting on the fireplace's hearthstones. She breathed in the aromatic incense, letting its soothing fragrance calm her thoughts. The tide of memory receded, replaced by a solid connection to the here... to the now... to this place in time and space.

By the time the wood burned down to bright coals filling the room with a soft light, her mind had cleared, fully anchored in the present.

It was time.

Grasping the EMF detector's chassis with both hands, she pointed the loop antenna toward the sandalwood smoke rising in lazy fragrant circles above the brazier. This was an aspect of the detector she had not divulged to detective Doyle. With it, she could do more than track the killer using his electromagnetic pattern discovered at the Hing Hay pavilion; she could visit the astral plane and see him.

A soft whine filled the room as the device calibrated itself to her electromagnetic signature. The glowing dial's black arrow snapped to full-on before settling once more on zero, as if waiting for her mental command to start searching the astral world.

The detector purred like a kitten as if recognizing her. Vibrations swept over her skin, and her entire body tingled. When she sensed her brain had linked with the detector, she tapped a black button that synched the device to the Schumann resonance and sent her mind into the astral realm.

Light hammered her, as if she'd opened a door from total darkness into bright day. She winced against the sharp pain in her eyes. Slowly, her brain tuned more completely to the existence of this other world. The brightness faded, and she saw the realm as a place of individual points of light, as many as stars in the night sky. Each one resonated with the energy of another human in touch with this other reality.

She marveled at the number of people who visited this occult domain. Many did so only while asleep. These people were faint, motionless stars scattered across the plane's paranormal cosmos — sleepwalkers experiencing nightmarish fantasies or pleasant reveries, and lucid dreamers who exercised some control over their dream characters, narrative, and environment but were not in a fully conscious state.

Brighter stars were people who, like Khoury, had summoned enough mental power to enter the other world while awake. They roamed across the darkness, pale comets questing for answers to eternity's greatest secrets, or merely observing the real world from which the mirrored image of Earth was drawn.

But, the glories of this astral firmament were pulsars, their electromagnetic radiation gleaming beacons. These individuals accessed the unlimited power of the astral plane to visit any place in the world and accomplish feats impossible to the ordinary human in daily life.

She studied these brilliant points of light, seeking the resonance she had picked up at the Grand Pavilion in Hing Hay Park. A powerful mind like the killer's would be easy to distinguish among all these other stars if he were here this night.

Khoury swallowed against the risk she was taking. Though she had linked with this other world many times, she had never spent more than a few hours in actual astral travel. In her brief forays, she had learned to recognize the types of players who visited here but not well enough to understand the great sweeping powers of the place. In some ways, she was worse than a neophyte. She knew just enough to get into trouble but not enough to protect herself.

The man pursuing vengeance had a powerful mind, and it was

quite possible he would sense her intrusion and come for her. If that happened, she had no choice but go back through the door she had stepped through to her home, where her physical body resided.

Steeling herself against this danger, Khoury waited, apprehensive but determined. She masked her intent by mellowing her presence to appear as a sleeper present only in a dream state and not really active. Several bright stars swung by but did not pay any attention to her.

She had begun to think the murderer wouldn't show, when a nova lit up the astral plane. The killer's angry vehemence careened by her with a suffocating brightness. Several dim points of light blinked out as he roared past, sleepers jolted out of their dreams by the nightmarish, lethal anger emanating from his etheric body.

Dampening her energy imprint without breaking her link to the astral plane, Khoury allowed herself to be drawn along, though she couldn't be sure he didn't see her shadowy form bobbing in his wake.

43

After a while, she sensed a difference in his emotions than from his attack on Willie Fong. Before, the need for vengeance had filled him with a rage that thirsted for obliteration of the men who destroyed his family. This time, remorse tinged his actions. Khoury sensed he had embarked on a mission he felt compelled to undertake but did not relish as he had with the other killings.

She followed him to a home overlooking the Fremont Cut, part of the waterway connecting Seattle's Lake Union to Puget Sound. The night was Elysian — the air calm, the moon a shining jewel above the Olympic Peninsula.

The man's astral self stopped outside an open first-floor window. Khoury peeked inside and saw an elderly Asian woman sitting calmly in an armchair near a fire. A cup of tea rested on a coffee table beside her. She looked up from the book she was reading and stared directly at the vengeful wraith. "I've been expecting you," she said.

He floated into the house and hovered near the fireplace. Khoury followed, staying in corner shadows unaffected by the fire. The man's anger appeared to make him oblivious to everyone except his prey. If the woman sensed Khoury, she let nothing show.

Though old, the woman's face had not been ravaged by time and still held the soft beauty of her youth. Her smile filled the space between them with peace and love, and she said without rancor or fear to the intruder, "You are the ghost killer."

The man jerked in surprise at her calm demeanor. Confusion weakened the angry halo obscuring his features, though a glowing rage still washed out most of his face, so Khoury couldn't distinguish more than passionate blue eyes, blazing with fury at the memory of the triads who had wronged him. "My family deserves justice. My little girls deserve—." Rage choked off his voice.

Khoury stifled a gasp at the overwhelming pain that radiated from the killer as he remembered his loved ones. She made herself as small as possible in a tiny niche beside the fireplace.

"The Dragons must pay for what they did to my family." Ghostly images of the man's loved ones projected into the room, two little girls and a man. "The dragons are a plague that must be stopped so they never do it to any others. You must not stop me", he said in a tone that pleaded with the old woman to let him continue his path of vengeance and he would let her live.

"I must stop you before your form of justice brings harm to innocents," the old woman said.

"My little girls were innocent. Where is justice for them?"

"Justice awaits everyone in the next world."

The man shook his head. "They will have justice in this world."

The wraith sent out a tendril of glowing energy toward the old woman, who began to chant.

Khoury drew in a sharp breath. The melodious voice sounded like the rustle of wind through cedar trees in her village back home. But that was not the source of her awe. With each singsong word, motes rose from the book as if a mini whirlwind were scouring the page and forming the letters into a thin veil between the old woman and the ghost killer.

The attack struck the barrier, crackled, and snapped back at him.

He reeled from the impact. He lashed out with a bolt of lightning. It rebounded and struck the fireplace near Khoury's hiding place, sending stone chips into the room.

The old woman smiled. "Unlike your victims, I am not without skills in this realm. I will stop you so you cannot kill again."

Her opposition enraged him, and any vestiges of remorse sloughed away from his astral being. Lamps exploded throughout the room, sending it into a darkness cut feebly by the fire's dying embers. For a heartbeat, the old woman's aura shown faintly behind the gauzy protection of her veil of energy. And the room was ablaze with the killer's stark silver light of vengeance as he drew in more power from the house's electrical grid. His blue eyes disappeared behind the blinding glare, and his form compressed into a blazing tiger readying to leap on its prey.

Khoury didn't see how his strike could fail. The amount of energy he possessed would smash through the old woman's defenses and kill her. She had to stop him, even if it meant putting herself in harm's way. Gritting her teeth, she drifted away from the safe shadows of her hideaway and came to rest between the two combatants. "Stop! She's not your enemy."

The killer turned his wrath on her. "You!" he cried, hurling the word like a knife.

The familiar tone startled Khoury, and, in that frightening moment, she thought once more she should know him. The way he stood, the way he commanded the power of the astral realm, felt strangely familiar. Then, the flash of insight was torn away as his anger fell upon her. An unrelenting roar filled her head. She staggered against the fireplace and collapsed on the floor. An unseen pressure crushed her into the carpet.

Khoury's mind was frozen from more than fear. The killer's overwhelming desire for vengeance compressed her thoughts. Pain bore down on her, filling her skull until her skin tightened and eyes swelled, and she feared her astral body would burst apart. When she thought she could endure no more, and the sweet deliverance of death was but a moment away, through the terrifying noise, a gentle but strong whisper sheltered her from the worst of the psychic onslaught. The wracking pain slackened, and she heard words clearly like a light in a cave-in showing the way out. She could make out the voice. It was the old woman urging her — "Get up.... Now... run!"

The awful pressure pinning her eased, and Khoury floated unsteadily to her feet. Her exit from the astral plane was a door ajar. It opened onto the soft light of her living room, cast by the brazier's glowing sandalwood embers. She saw her physical body sitting in full lotus, delicate hands grasping the looped antenna of the electromagnetic field detector. She reached for the opening. All she needed was to set one foot inside, and the astral plane would disappear behind her like a dream fading with the morning sun.

The killer saw it too, and he was faster. He fashioned a lightning bolt in his left hand and hurled it at her.

Khoury was still too far from the exit and knew she was dead. But before the bolt struck, the old woman extended her shield, and the energy deflected into the room, slamming into the coffee table. The teapot exploded, and jasmine perfumed the air.

The effort weakened the old woman. The killer turned on her and began battering the now thin shield with an unrelenting barrage of electrical bolts.

"Go," the old woman cried. She wasted no more breath but bent to the task of defending herself.

Khoury stepped through the door in the same moment she let go of the EMF device. The effect was not instantaneous. Some of her residual energy still occupied the astral plane and held the door open. She saw the killer and the old woman locked in combat. Her shield rapidly weakened, and triumph blazed through the man's astral body.

Then the door swung shut, and the scene disappeared as if a blanket had smothered a fire. Khoury found herself in the safety of her living room, alone, in the fetal position, rocking beside the brazier against the cold rage of the man's vengeance.

Her paralysis lasted seconds. "I have to save her," she said. She rose unsteadily and clutched the fireplace's mantel for balance. Then, grabbing a pistol-like object from the table, she rushed outside to her car. She spotted the tan Volvo parked beside a fire hydrant away from the streetlight. The driver hunched down to obscure his face, but not before Khoury recognized the hawk-nosed profile matching her own. Her brother had found where she lived, which could only mean trouble. She had lied to the detective. She wasn't sure she could handle her brother.

She couldn't think of that now. The old woman was in danger.

44

Madison Park

Never go to bed angry. It's Pop's favorite advice. If taken, a lot of people would never sleep at all.... Maybe it's why there are so many murders.

I left Hagler in the den, hoping he'd talk to Cassandra. Deep down, I knew they belonged together.

Me... I was beginning to wonder if I belonged with anyone.

Pamela apparently thought so, or maybe she had called me to bed to give our relationship one last shot.

I stood by the sweeping staircase leading up to the second floor, pondering the state of affairs for more time than was prudent to keep her waiting. Finally, I climbed each step as if I were Indiana Jones negotiating a chamber full of booby traps. The bedroom door stood partly open, and I went in, closing it silently behind me. The wine bottle was on her nightstand — empty. The bed, on the other hand, was half full... if you're an optimist... and twice as big as it needed to be if you're an engineer.

I was caught in the middle, so I chose the option of undressing, slipping under the covers, and waiting.

Pamela stared at me from her side, arms crossed. I'm a detective, but the heart of an angry girlfriend is the hardest rock in this world, and I can find no clue of how to make things right when I've erred. So, the silence went on and on until my phone rang. Pamela's eyes narrowed to dark points that warned, if I answered it, I could kiss sleeping here tonight good-bye.

"It's work," I said, as if that should smooth things over. It didn't. I picked up anyway. The voice on the other end was loud enough for Pamela to hear. That didn't help any, because it was female.

"The killer is going to strike again," Khoury said, her voice strangely calm, as if she were reading a brochure for a cruise in the Mediterranean.

"How do you know this?" I asked.

"I used my EMF to track him. If I can get there in time, I can stop him."

Her unperturbed manner sent warning signals through my gut, and my mind whirled with scattered thoughts and impressions of this strange woman — psychic... liar... physicist... liar. *Yeah, I couldn't trust her.* Still, what if she was right? I mean, I couldn't let her go after this guy alone, right?

"If you try to stop him, he'll kill you."

"I have to try," she said.

"What makes you think you can stop him?"

"I have a way."

Ghostbusting aside, I had Pamela glaring at me. The angry disbelief on her face at my showing concern for another woman and not her was undeniable. I was stuck in a dilemma that made the space "between a rock and a hard place" a spa.

"Give me the address. I'll meet you there." Khoury hesitated. "Look," I said, "if there was ever a moment you want me to trust you, it's now."

She gave me an address. I didn't have to write it down. I recognized it. "Wait till I get there," I ordered, but the line was already dead.

"I have to go, babe," I said to Pamela.

"Cassandra needs to see you," she said, her voice as icy as her stare.

"It's the case. An informant has a lead." I pushed out of bed and began to dress. Maybe I should have been more forthcoming. Maybe it was the middle of the night, or maybe the lack of Risperdal in my system was letting my darker, self-absorbed side show, but goddamn it, Pamela's attitude was beginning to piss me off. In the year we had been together, I had never given her any reason to doubt my affection for her. That alone should have earned me some goodwill points and the benefit of the doubt. But her stare and angry tone made it clear she wasn't about to give me anything but crap. I could think of only one word: shrew.

Maybe she sensed my attitude. She dug in her heels, literally. I could see them pushing hard into the mattress. She twisted the covers in her fists as if strangling something while she looked fixedly at my neck. "Walk out that door, and don't bother coming home," she grated. "And you'd better take Hagler with you."

If you're a guy reading this, you probably know the routine, either through personal experience or a friend. I had a choice: stay and work things out, or do my job and come home to my things on the lawn. I would have gone even if I didn't believe Khoury. The chilly room and freezing bed was more than enough incentive to leave the house and stay away.

"Send my things to the precinct," I said. Secretly, all bravado aside, I hoped we could patch things up. I loved Pamela. I really did. I loved being a detective even more.

I woke Hagler and told him about the murder happening. He rolled his eyes, pulled the sheet over his head, and said, "Call me when you have a body."

Khoury's premonition didn't work, so I told him what Pamela had threatened.

"For real?" he said.

"For real."

He got up. Nothing like a woman's scorn to motivate a man to movement. The clock was ticking a lot faster than proverbially, so without letting him put his pants and shoes on, I rushed him out of the house... without socks too. We were through the community's security gate almost before the red-striped bar had lifted.

"You believe this psychic enough to leave a warm bed in the middle of the night and chase ghosts?" Hagler asked with the same bewilderment my own mind shouted at me. My gut screamed louder than both of them. I believed her more than I believed in the sanctity of my relationship with Pamela. "It's complicated," I said.

"It's fucked," Hagler answered.

"That too."

45

Fremont

T he small community of Fremont lies along the northern side of the canal connecting Puget Sound to Lake Union. During the counter-culture revolution of the 1960s and 1970s, it adopted the title, the People's Republic of Fremont... until it became gentrified, and low and middle-income people were priced out of living there. God bless our economy.

Now it's best known for its sculpture, Waiting for the Interurban. Made from recycled aluminum, it commemorates the light rail line that used to connect downtown Seattle with its far-flung neighborhoods. The piece depicts six people and a dog with a human face. Legend says the face on the dog belongs to Arman Napoleon Stepanian, dubbed the unofficial mayor of Fremont at the time. Rumor has it the sculptor and the so-called mayor wasted no love on each other, which goes to prove the old adage, never piss off an artist.

From the address in Fremont and Khoury's description of the old woman, I knew it had to be Auntie Toy's home. I couldn't figure out why the killer would target her. She was a harmless old fortuneteller who literally wouldn't hurt a fly. Karma, she called it.

I drove with lights and sirens and still didn't beat Khoury to the house. I found her on the front steps, head down, crying.

The front door stood open. Auntie Toy never locked it. She said if people needed something, they could come in and take it. Not that anyone would, given her ties to Uncle Lo and the Seattle tongs.

Let's get one thing straight I should have mentioned early on. The Seattle tongs controlled a lot of the harmless fun the city council and the mayor thought should be outlawed. So, yeah, they broke the law, but they weren't vicious like the I-5 Dragon Triads. They wouldn't cut your hands off if you owed them money, and they sure as hell wouldn't kill you if you crossed them. Even so, no one risked the wrath of the tongs, so Auntie Toy was safe in her unlocked home. Everyone, and I mean everyone, knew this... except the bastard who left her bloodless corpse on the floor of her living room.

Hagler and I examined the crime scene. Every light had exploded, leaving slivers of glass everywhere. It appeared Auntie Toy had put up a fight, though nothing like the triads. No shots fired, no busted-out car windows, no bludgeoning. A chair and coffee table were over-turned. Tea stained the plush carpet. It smelled of jasmine, her favorite. From the condition of her body, she had done a better job than the Dragons defending herself. Unlike their battered corpses, she didn't have a mark on her. She also had a smile on her face.

I left Hagler to call the ME's office to get the Sparrowhawk brothers down here and went back outside to wait for the black and whites to arrive while I spoke to Khoury. She stopped crying and wiped her eyes. She held a book in her hands. I took it gently from her. I recognized the *I Ching*. Not that I could read it. The book was beyond old, the characters archaic. The oily feel of the leather binding made me think it belonged in the rare-books room of a library and not in Auntie's home.

"The old woman was reading it," Khoury said.

"Do you know who she was?" I asked.

She shook her head.

"Auntie Toy. She used the *I Ching* to read fortunes for people."

Khoury laughed. Not hysterically but with the odd, comical laugh of a person who can barely believe what they witnessed. "It's not funny. It's just... the *I Ching*, at least among Chinese, was considered a powerful tool in sorcery... black magic." Khoury bit her lip. "She used it to save my life."

"You were here when this happened?"

"I was, and I wasn't."

She must have realized how ambiguous she sounded, because she started to explain, when two black and whites converged, parking in the traditional V shape in front of the house. I motioned the officers over and told them to secure the area and begin a canvass. One of them was Sandra Liu. She took me aside.

"What?" I asked, looking back at Khoury. I wanted to hear her story before she clammed up.

"The tan Volvo with the Arab driving. I saw it speeding away as I approached the house."

"Thanks," I said.

I went back over to where Khoury sat, her body rigid, lips pressed in a firm line of determination not to move, forcing the officers to file around her into the home. "Come with me," I said. We went inside into Auntie Toy's kitchen. It was spotless — all the utensils carefully arranged, pots hanging from a cooking rack over a huge six-burner stove. I wondered if she ever actually cooked here. "Tell me what happened," I asked gently.

Khoury laid it all out for me — using her homemade EMF to find the killer on the astral plane, fleeing, driving here. I let her speak without interrupting. "I didn't get here in time. I —" She choked back tears. "Auntie Toy saved my life," she repeated.

The story, fantastical without a shred of proof, except for the bloodless, dead woman on the floor of the living room, begged to be ridiculed. But by the way Khoury spoke, the tone in her voice, I would have sworn she hadn't made up any of it. She had been here when the killer struck.

On the other hand, she left out the part about her brother. I asked, "What about Mahir driving away from the scene? When were you going to tell me about him?"

She blanched at the question. "He had nothing to do with this. It's a family—"

"A family matter. I know. But it's still very convenient and suspicious he was here when Auntie Toy died."

"She was dead when I got here. He followed me, so he couldn't be your killer."

True, if I believed her.

Hagler stood in the doorway. I motioned him in. He motioned me to join him. "Don't leave the house," I cautioned Khoury.

"There's nowhere I can go," she answered.

That was true too.

In the living room, the Sparrowhawk twins were putting Auntie Toy into a body bag. By the reverent manner in which they handled her remains, they knew the importance of treating her right. CSI Sheila Cummings took pictures, which was all she could do since, like the other crime scenes, there were no forensics — no blood, fingerprints, hair samples, DNA under the fingernails — and the only witness had seen the attacker while camped out on the astral plane. My report was going to read like an Anne Rice novel.

I put those thoughts on hold and concentrated on Hagler. I didn't have to ask him the cause of death. It was the same as the others. "When did Auntie Toy die?"

"Skin is still warm... Within half an hour." He looked at the kitchen. "She could be telling the truth, and her brother didn't have anything to do with this."

He didn't state the obvious, but I did. "Besides, how do you drain all the blood out of a body and not leave any clues behind."

The Sparrowhawk brothers eyed each other. "Sasquatch," they murmured in unison. Hagler didn't respond, "Vampires," for which I was grateful. I might have shot all three. It had been eighteen hours since my last Risperdal dose.

Auntie Toy's death put a whole new emphasis on the case. Dead gangbangers I could live with, but Auntie was a beloved character in

Chinatown. I had no idea how to break this to Uncle Lo. Not only to him. The other tong leaders would demand justice. If they suspected the I-5 Dragons had anything to do with her murder, a war with the triads was all but inevitable.

My only witness swore the killing happened on the astral plane. Was she protecting her brother? One way to find out. I pulled Sheila Cummings from her meaningless task of documenting non-existing evidence. "Check the street cams, especially the routes from North-gate in the last hour."

"What am I looking for?"

I gave her the description of the tan Volvo, license plate, and the driver. I gave her Khoury's license plate too. "See if it's following a silver Mercedes."

"On it." She pulled out an iPad and started at once. Eager as I was to get back to my prime suspect, I waited. It didn't take long. Aurora at 80th Street, both cars, the Volvo following the Mercedes as it sped through a red light toward Auntie Toy's home. The time stamp was at the time of death. Neither of them could have been involved in Auntie Toy's murder.

I headed toward the kitchen, when Malvern's bald head, brow furrowed in disgust, thrust through the front door. The rest of him followed — dress blues, polished shoes. He held a long twist of red licorice in his left hand; another dangled from his mouth. He chewed quickly, as if trying to make sense of what he saw. "I don't like being dragged out of bed in the middle of the night, Doyle," he greeted me. "This better not be what I think it is."

"It's not," I assured him.

"The deceased is Auntie Toy, isn't it?" he said, clearly disagreeing with my assessment of the situation.

"Yes, boss."

He swallowed the wad of licorice, glaring at me. "What makes you think it isn't payback by the I-5 Dragons?"

"It's not the triad's style. Same MO as the others. Same killer."

He grunted. "Good to know the ghost killer isn't going after one side."

I winced at the name. Some overeager, smartass reporter at the *Seattle Times* had used my facetious name for the killer, undoubtedly thinking it was a clever moniker. "The press is going to be here any minute," I reminded Malvern.

He grunted again. "I'll handle the press," he said. "You find me the killer." He stalked out of the house.

I went back into the kitchen. Khoury hadn't strayed from where I left her next to the stove. "Come with me," I said.

"You arresting me?" she asked.

I shook my head. "I want to talk somewhere else.... away from all of this before the press arrives."

46

Beth's Café

B eth's Café is the quintessential American diner known for its greasy-
spoon cuisine. The owners proudly say so on their website, and a
signboard above the entrance flings down at every passerby, "I'd be vegan
too if bacon grew on trees." Beth's is home to the twelve-egg omelet and
bottomless hash browns. They have a defibrillator on the wall next to the
cash register, as a joke... I think. It's also open twenty-four hours and serves
exceptional coffee.

I left Hagler with the body. We had logistics to coordinate — where to
sleep since Pamela's house was off limits — but those could wait.
Before I spoke with Uncle Lo and gave him the sad-bad news, I
needed to know everything Khoury knew about Auntie Toy's killer.
Yeah, maybe I was beginning to believe her. I mean, when the
mundane has been eliminated, the unusual and the impossible
become the next best suspects.

The awning at Beth's Café lit up Seattle's dark night by
proclaiming the name of the restaurant in brilliant red and blue

lights. We missed the midnight crowd, and the only people in the place aside from the staff were a gaggle of University of Washington football players at the counter, egging on a lineman attacking a twelve-egg omelet on a bed of crispy hash browns.

A waitress with more tattoos than a sailor, spiked green-tinted hair, and a ring in her nose, told us her name was Nancy and took our orders of coffee.

Khoury looked askance at the young woman as she swayed back toward the kitchen. "I've never gotten used to the way some American women dress," she said. "She looks clownish."

"Nancy," I called out. Our waitress turned. "What do you do for a living?"

"Landscape architect," she answered and disappeared behind the counter.

I said to Khoury, "Nobody who works here passes for normal."

"Is that why you prefer this place?" Khoury asked. "Because you don't have to pass for normal?"

I shrugged. Maybe she was right.

Nancy brought our coffees, no cream or sugar, and left without a comment. At 2:00 in the morning, no one was going to disturb us. Privacy was something everyone in the place respected.

I asked Khoury to describe the killer.

Again, she painted a picture of a man furious at a personal loss. The only distinct feature she described was his blazing blue eyes.

"What loss?" I asked.

"It's not the same as watching a cinema," she said, her English good but not idiomatic. "What I saw were two small children and an older man floating with him. They were joined by a blue thread of light, and yet, they were not... real."

"And this guy is real?" I asked, unable to hide the smirk in my voice. The case might have entered the impossible zone, but I wasn't a believer yet.

Khoury didn't seem to mind. "To the non-believer, the astral world is something to scoff at. Those of us who experience it can untangle the substance from the ephemeral. This man is real. He lives. The three individuals connected to him have already passed on. He carries their images with him because he loves them and can't let them go, so they follow him on the astral plane of existence."

She paused, and I sensed she was holding something back. "Look, I can't get to the bottom of whatever the hell is going on here if you hold out on me. So, give."

Khoury furled her lower lip in her teeth. "In spite of all the science, the astral world still involves a lot of nuance and speculation. The way of explaining the other world is sometimes like explaining art to a novice. The man I saw wants to join his family, but he wants to avenge their deaths before he does."

"What does he look like?"

"Pale, tall, American, middle-aged, dark hair, blue eyes."

Once again, all this otherworldly hocus-pocus pointed to Andrew Chapman — a brain-dead suspect with a dead husband and two little adopted Vietnamese girls, also dead — if you believed Khoury's story. I remembered seeing him at Harborview's ICU two nights after the murder of his family. He had pale blue eyes. They didn't sparkle. They were as flat as a dead fish. The attending doctor assured me he would never wake up.

"You just described a suspect I happen to know for a fact is in a persistent vegetative state and incapable of any thought let alone traveling on the astral plane. So, how do you explain that with your mystical hocus-pocus?"

"I can't, except to say things are not always as they seem."

It would have been a much more satisfying answer if she had smirked or given me some other hint that she was lying. But she sat stoically across from me in all seriousness.

I hid my disappointment. Everything had dialed back to zero, and I wasn't any closer to solving the mystery. I glanced at Khoury and switched to Arabic. "Why didn't you quit the case the other day when I was rude to you?"

She shrugged. "Your future is not what you think it is, Mr. Doyle. You're going to need a friend when this is over."

"Don't we all," I muttered.

I checked the time. Nearly 3:00. Some of the staff put on coats, including Nancy. They hugged each other and left. The early morning shift would be arriving in a few minutes. A lot of people hit Beth's before work.

I left a large tip, thanks to William Chen. "Let's go," I said.

"Where are we going?" Khoury asked.

"Back to the crime scene. You can get your car and go home."

"What about you?"

Yeah, what about me? I scrubbed my face with both hands. My left still smelled of jasmine tea. I had an unpleasant task to perform. With Sandra Liu at Auntie Toy's house, chances were, Uncle Lo already knew about her murder. Still, I owed the old man a personal visit to tell him what happened. I sighed and said, "I have to tell someone the very unpleasant news about Auntie Toy."

"Maybe I should go with you. I can tell him what I saw," she said matter-of-factly, as if she hadn't witnessed a brutal killing.

Yet, behind that stoic demeanor sat a woman with both hands wrapped around a cup of coffee as if warding off an unaccustomed chill on this warm August night. Behind her eyes was the same perplexing dread she exhibited at the Hidden Corner after her foray into the astral realm at the Hing Hay pavilion. I got the feeling Khoury was afraid to go home alone. "This killer got you spooked?"

She bit her lip again. I noticed she wasn't wearing lipstick, which matched her story of leaving the house in a hurry. Maybe, on a normal night, I would have waited for her to get her act together then tell me what was bothering her. But tonight wasn't normal by any means. Too many unknowns made my brain hurt. "Give," I said.

She bristled at my tone. "I'm not hiding anything about my brother."

"I know that. There's something you're puzzled about, even scared."

She studied the black hollowness of her coffee mug. "It's the killer. Right before I left the astral plane, he yelled 'You!' at me like he knew me." She looked away, looked back. "I don't see how he could know me. And yet, I feel as if I should know him."

"A feeling?"

"A feeling." She took a deep breath. "I'm afraid he can find me, and if he does, and I'm not prepared, he will kill me."

"Jesus!" I drained what was left of my coffee and signaled Nancy to hit us again. I waited until she left. "Earlier, you said something about being able to stop him."

"Yes, if he doesn't catch me by surprise."

I made one of those spur-of-the-moment decisions that usually has the rest of the squad room snickering. "All right, you're with me."

47

Good Luck Noodle House

The *Good luck Noodle House isn't a 24/7/365 place like Beth's Café, but it stays open into the wee hours most mornings, and later on a Friday night. Chinatown never really sleeps. If you have the cash and the stomach for it, you can get whatever you want, though my uncle Jack once told me, "What you want is not always what you need." He also said, "Never give a sword to a man who can't dance."*

Uncle Lo's place of business was lit up and empty. A lone waitress was sleeping in a booth by the door. She woke when Khoury and I entered and said in heavily accented English, "You want to see menu?"

"We're here to see Uncle Lo," I said in Mandarin. The young girl gaped at me. I repeated it in Cantonese, and she scurried into the kitchen.

We didn't wait long. Lo appeared in a simple black tunic. His eyes were red from crying. As I expected, news of Auntie Toy's death had already reached him. We sat down without a word. Tea arrived right away along with dim sum. The waitress fled once more into the kitchen.

I introduced Khoury to him. He bowed his head politely but didn't extend his hand in greeting. He said in Cantonese, "Why bring this woman to meet me? We have important things to discuss about the triad killings and Auntie Toy." His voice broke on her name. The two had been more than business partners over the years.

I waited for him to gather himself and answered, "She has information I am sure will prove interesting if not useful to you and the tongs."

Lo eyed Khoury. To her credit, she didn't straighten up as if trying to pass muster. She returned his gaze with a look that went beyond "I see you" and into "I know you."

Uncle Lo drew in a soft breath, bowed his head with respect this time and switched back to English. "What kind of information?"

I nodded at Khoury. "Tell him what you told me."

She did.

I sat back and sipped tea. My eyes on Khoury, I barely noticed anything else inside the restaurant. Hearing the tale about the astral plane and the man who killed Auntie Toy a second time reinforced my apprehension over facing forces I had no idea how to defeat. Maybe the lack of Risperdal caused my brain to go on tangents I normally wouldn't give a first glance to let alone a second, but as early morning edged its way out of night, I had come to believe I was caught in some dark urban fantasy, and my usual Sam Spade attitude wasn't going to cut it.

Khoury finished, and what Lo did next cemented my fears. Sure, his eyes were red, but the tears had long since dried and his voice calmed, as if he'd expected this turn of events. Maybe he had. His conversation with Auntie Toy two nights ago hadn't just been about the *I Ching* or smugglers bars. Auntie Toy had seen the future, or maybe a possible future, that included her death at the hands of the ghost killer. Uncle Lo pulled a small leather-bound book from the sleeve of his tunic. "Auntie Toy came here this evening and gave me this before she went home. It's her personal diary."

He opened the book to the last few pages. They were filled with Chinese characters. I can read a few street signs, airport stuff, etcetera, but that's all. I shook my head.

Lo frowned at my lack of refinement. As far as he was concerned, I was an ignorant barbarian who just happened to speak the language of the middle kingdom. (He might have been born and educated in the US and a genius in business, but he embodied the millennia-old belief that the Chinese occupied the space between heaven and the rest of the planet.)

He translated the last entries for our benefit. Apparently, the night before, Auntie Toy had seen the triad killer. Her diary's description fit the man lying in Greenbrier Nursing home, brain dead and body kept alive by machines.

48

West Precinct

M*y Pops has a favorite saying: "When all else fails, read the directions." Only, what can you do when there aren't any directions? Or worse, what if Ikea sent the wrong kit, and you're holding up a part A that doesn't exist in your universe?*

"Weird" didn't even begin to fit the Dr. Strange universe I'd found myself in as I sat at my desk staring out the window at another cloud-less August morning in Seattle. Out on Elliot Bay, a pair of wind surfers ripped across the water, and a kite surfer hung in the air with the grace of a trapeze artist working without a net.

Malvern glared at me from his office. He held a swizzle of red licorice in both hands as if he intended to garrote me with it. I had filled him in on what happened last night, down to the details of Khoury's run-in with what the entire squad now called the ghost killer. "Freakin' ludicrous" was the kindest thing Malvern said about my working theory about the case. When I reminded him he had set me on this track with Khoury in the first place, he shouted me out of his office.

I didn't blame him. Khoury and Auntie Toy's explanations linked the killer to the murder of Chapman's family a year ago, establishing motive. They gave eyewitness accounts, showing opportunity. And finally, the electromagnetic power available in the astral plane provided the means to drain the blood from all the victims. Neat, open and shut. Problem was, I had a guy who couldn't possibly have done the murders, because he was bedridden at Greenbrier Nursing Home... brain dead. All the doctors said so.

(Yeah, I know, I'm repeating myself — a killer who can't possibly be the killer. In the moment, I hoped if I said it aloud enough times, the only working theory would magically disappear, and some deranged lunatic would step forward, admit to doing a public service by killing gangbangers, and apologize for being overzealous in going after Auntie Toy. If only.)

Fortunately or not, depending on the point of view, my repetitious spiral into the paranormal world of murder was interrupted by a separate though equally perplexing and disheartening downward spiral. This one personal.

Dr. Herschel called. Somehow, he'd persuaded Mama to get an MRI of her brain. He'd found what he'd hoped he wouldn't. Mama definitely had frontotemporal dementia. Cancer was something surgeons could cut out. FTD was incurable.

I could hear the sigh in his voice. "We don't have a baseline scan to compare this one with, but given the amount of damage we see, your mother is deteriorating rapidly. She's in no shape to care for your father."

I tried to talk around the lump in my throat, couldn't.

Herschel picked up the slack. "She'll need to be institutionalized to protect her from herself, and you'll need to find a full-time home health worker to care for your father. I'm sorry," he added and finished the call with, "I'll check in on your parents later this evening."

Yesterday, I'd looked into the worst-case scenario, which this morning had become the only scenario. The cost of institutionalizing Mama was a hundred grand a year. A full-time health care worker for Pops was another hundred grand. Because of Medicare rules, the government would not pay for all of both parents' health care costs until they'd gone through all of their savings, including the house. I checked their bank balances, and what they could reasonably expect with a reverse mortgage. The money would run out in three years. And the care available for the destitute after that was not pretty.

(Maybe you're thinking about all that money in the Police Tong's secret Cayman accounts. It would be easy for me to use it. And while at it, I could find myself a nice place to live, with a maid to clean up after myself and a nicer ride than the thirty-one-year-old Toyota truck I drive.)

No, I wasn't going to be the first to slide down that slippery slope.

Hagler called. Maybe he had something from Auntie Toy's body that would point to a theory of what happened that didn't involve ghost killers. If only.

49

E ver notice how life is a shit sandwich? It goes down a lot easier with a lot of bread. Yeah, that's a lame metaphor. But what's even more lame is the press giving serial killers what they think are cool names. In this case, ghost killer. It's as if they want to glamorize these people.

Americans lap up murder like cats at a saucer of milk. Maybe it's a genetic thing that has followed us through the ages. The Roman Empire had the bloody spectator sport of gladiators fighting to the death in the Coliseum. Europe had bear pits, and whole villages turned out to watch witches burn at the stake. America in the twenty-first century isn't so different. With crime dramas devoted to serial killers as well as tons of documentaries on killing, and more mass shootings than all other nations combined, we glamorize the spectacle of murder, and...

Not taking the Risperdal for twenty-four hours narrowed my focus, some of it in good ways. It also made me liable to rant, unless I consciously stopped myself.

I quashed my philippic (lack of Risperdal in my system also

means I seize on unusual words) when I walked into the cold room where Hagler had Auntie Toy's body stretched out on the stainless-steel table. He'd already finished stitching up the transverse incisions on her chest.

Auntie Toy had made a lot of money for herself over the years, which was why she could afford a place in the gentrified neighborhood of Fremont. Yet, in the end, all the money and power hadn't helped her stave off death. But it hadn't corrupted her either. If Dr. Khoury was to be believed, Auntie Toy had saved her life by shielding her from the ghost killer. Yeah, I'm using that lame-ass name. And if I run into the ass who coined it, I'll tell him so.

Auntie Toy barely filled half the table. She looked terribly small for a woman who had been a driving force in Seattle's tongs for so many years. She also had a peaceful look on her face and a Giaconda smile that would have given Da Vinci fits. I couldn't help but wonder what secrets that smile hid.

"Tell me you called me down here because you have something," I said.

Hagler took off his glasses and cleaned the lenses. They were already spotless. He had the habit of doing that when he wanted to share something important. "Not all the blood was drained from her body."

"The killer was interrupted?"

He shrugged. "That could be one explanation, or if Ms. Khoury is correct, maybe Auntie Toy's fight with him on the astral plane weakened his power enough that he couldn't complete his MO." He pointed to a quart of blood on a cart next to him. "I'll send it to the lab. Maybe analysis can tell us something useful."

A seemingly invincible killer who could be stopped. That sounded encouraging.

Hagler put his glasses back on and asked, "Do you believe our Lebanese psychic?"

My turn to shrug. Her explanation sounded better than vampires or Sasquatch, but did I believe her? I wanted to. The traffic cams had cleared her and her brother of involvement in the killings, but something hinky between them cast a lingering shadow of doubt on her story and made me suspicious.

Family, I sighed silently. *Can't live with 'em, can't shoot 'em.* It reminded me of my own family troubles. I had to arrange care for Pops and Mama. "You were right, Mel, about my mom. She has frontotemporal dementia. Dr. Herschel confirmed it today."

The sudden change in direction of the conversation caught Hagler off guard. He fiddled with a rib cutter for several seconds before answering, "I'm sorry, Jack. I wish something could be done."

"You know of a reliable home health care company?" I asked.

"Why ask me?" Hagler said.

"You're a doctor."

"I'm an ME, Jack. I deal with dead bodies, not living ones." He cocked his head to one side. "It's a lot safer." He grimaced, and I could practically hear angry tears in his breathing. Maybe the talk hadn't gone as well as he'd hoped.

"Did you call Cassie?" I asked.

"A little while ago. Looks like I'll be sleeping here at the morgue. What about you? Any luck with Pamela?"

"I'll stay with my parents tonight."

I walked out of the ME's office and headed for the Harborview ER, where nurse Geneva Bowen worked. She'd been adamant that Andrew Chapman wasn't the brain-dead vegetable doctors made him out to be. She'd also insisted he had nothing to do with the Chinatown murders.

I hung here for a moment because my mind, fracturing ever so slowly with the Risperdal clearing out of my system, was seizing on other suspects with the same single-mindedness I'd had as a six-year-old solving jigsaw puzzles. See, supposing I believed Khoury was telling the truth, I still wasn't ready to admit her theory of the crimes was right... even if it did neatly tie up motive, means, and opportunity. The problem was, I had no way to prove her claims. That left me with a humdrum, old-fashioned flesh, blood-and-bone murderer to find.

And with traffic cams clearing Khoury and her brother, I had to come up with a new suspect. Fortunately, one popped up on my radar — Geneva Bowen. After my run-in with her at the Harborview ER a couple of days ago, I'd done some checking on her. She had a spotless record as a nurse and never had as much as a parking ticket. But she did have a dark moment in her past.

Two years ago, her niece — Andrea Bowen, whose father was a detective in Seattle's South Precinct — had been shot in a drive-by. She died in the Harborview ER with Geneva tending her. Some I-5 Dragons had been accused, but the charges were dropped for lack of evidence and witnesses who refused to testify. With no way to substantiate Khoury's disembodied-spirit hypothesis, Nurse Bowen was a human, real-world lead worth pursuing.

Harborview's emergency room was quiet for a Friday afternoon. Maybe it was the lull before the storm. The nurse behind the admitting desk told me Geneva had left for the day, citing personal reasons.

I didn't bother asking where she lived. Even if I showed my badge, they would have insisted on a court order. Maybe it was all the medical shows on TV, but hospitals were a lot stingier about giving out information than they used to be.

I walked outside under a bright afternoon sun sliding toward the peaks of the Olympic Mountains. A slight undercurrent of dampness chilling the air heralded the coming of autumn only a few weeks away. Rain would quickly follow. I had a couple of days left before McCrory's fishing boat sailed without me for the start of salmon season.

I still hadn't arranged care for my parents. I did a quick phone search for home health care companies that provided twenty-four-hour services for elderly couples with dementia. I found two and called the first one because it had a Care Bear in its logo. They agreed to meet me at my parents' home in half an hour. I still had no idea how I would pay for the service.

On my way to Ravenna, Uncle Lo called. He spoke in rapid Cantonese, his voice agitated, and without any of the usual pleasantries. "Jack, Auntie Toy's niece, Myrna, is missing."

"That's a missing person's case, Uncle Lo."

"I think you must look into it, Jack," he insisted. "She is nowhere around, vanished."

"Where does she work?" I asked.

"Greenbrier Nursing Home."

The word "bingo" went off in my head. It really did. No detective worth his salt made light of coincidences. "I'll look into it, Uncle Lo."

I was definitely going to Greenbrier tonight.

50

Madison Park

For a few weeks in August, when the sun is just above the western horizon, light filters through Seattle in angelic sparkles, proclaiming all is right with the world. If you're standing in the right place, you can see the effect on the Cascades to the east. It makes them look like mountains from a fairy tale. Not one of the original, dark Brothers Grimm fables where Hansel and Gretel get eaten by the witch, but a Hollywood fairy tale, where everything works out just right, and everyone lives happily ever after. Turn to the west, and the forests of Olympic Peninsula are cast in shadow, as if Mordor had risen and the time of humans on this planet was coming to an end. The dichotomy strikes you as a feral choice — life or death.

We each get to choose which way we face.

I was caught up in that choice while sitting in my thirty-one-year-old Toyota truck outside Pamela's home. Maybe I'm being overly dramatic, but with everything happening in my personal life, and with the ghost killer case, it seemed a whirlpool waited for me the moment I stepped out my car.

. . .

Earlier in the late afternoon I pulled into my parents' drive. Dr. Herschel was already inside. The home health care company's representative arrived a minute later. She was a middle-aged, Jewish woman, shorter than Mama. Turned out, she owned the company and did these visits personally. It was a nice touch and won me over. I was ready to sign on the dotted line before we entered the kitchen.

Dr. Herschel grilled the company owner on the needs of an elderly couple, one with a stroke and the other with dementia. My parents watched. I couldn't say if they were confused or not. Mama made chai and set out plates of naan and samosas as if she were hosting a party. Pops looked on from his wheelchair with a bored expression that said he'd rather be playing cribbage with Luis, who had arrived part way through the interview. He was there to spend the night.

"Darv," Mama said sweetly, setting her teacup on the table with extra care so as not to rattle the saucer or ripple the chai.

Maybe none of the others noticed, because it wasn't directed at them, but it seemed a pall had descended with the soft emphasis on my name. My chest tightened, and I felt like a little kid tiptoeing across a frozen pond, the ice brittle and creaking with each step.

"Why are you going to all this fuss with... with this nice Jewish woman to care for us? We're perfectly fine and don't need any help. Maybe you're the one with the problem and need full-time care." Her voice remained sweet, but her eyes narrowed, and her smile thinned.

My mind froze. I couldn't see how to stop her from revealing my secret to Luis and the Jewish lady with her next words.

Dr. Herschel interrupted. "As your and Henry's physician, I'm recommending you have full-time caretakers, Amrit," he said, using her first name and patting her hand reassuringly. "It's for the best."

Mama batted her eyes coquettishly. Pops snorted. He would have left to play cribbage with Luis then and there, but Dr. Herschel insisted he had to sign the agreement. In the end, Mama and Pops both signed because Dr. Herschel told them to, and they trusted him.

That hurt.

That was one reason I was sitting in my car outside Pamela's house instead of spending the night at my parents' home. At least she hadn't told security at the gate to shoot me on sight.

The house was inviting — brick and stone façade, high gabled roof, curtains pulled back on mullioned floor-to-ceiling windows, landscaped Japanese maples, beds of flowers and manicured lawn, stone walkways... a place where fairy tales came true. But staring at its upper-class wealth, I realized it wasn't really my fairy tale. Pamela owned the house, and I was a semi-permanent guest because I kept the bed warm.

Still, I had Mama and Pops to think about, and maybe Pamela could help in spite of the growing rift between us.

I had given up my rent-controlled apartment a year ago and in letting it go had signaled to Pamela I was serious about our relationship. That seemed a good place to start a conversation asking for her forgiveness.

Nothing says "I love you" like a text message. I know her number by heart. It was a thing I did to keep my mind sharp. I memorized all phone numbers. It really was faster than using speed dial. I punched in the Seattle area code, but my fingers betrayed me.

Cassandra answered with that contralto voice that tugged at my heartstrings every time I heard it. "This is a surprise, Darv. You call to tell me you can't follow through with the clinic?"

"No," I lied. I had been meaning to tell her she needed to ask Hagler. "A promise is a promise, Cass. I wanted to talk to you about Mel. He loves you, you know."

"Everybody loves somebody, sometimes," she said so flatly I winced.

"Yeah, but he loves you, and more importantly, you've never stopped loving him for a moment."

She hesitated, then said, "You take your Risperdal today? You seem uncommonly sure of yourself."

I still hadn't refilled my prescription, and my eyes were steady as a rock instead of darting all over the place like a honeybee buzzing from flower to flower. My thinking had sharpened to the same degree as it had been in elementary school when I solved every puzzle in the building on the day my first-grade teacher, Mrs. Baines, called my parents to tell them she thought I should be checked out. That was the first time I met Dr. Herschel. Answers to life's hardest questions hung in the air in front of me. The only problem was, they were written in code, and I didn't have the key. *No worries*, I told myself. *You'll find it soon. You just have to keep looking for the missing puzzle piece.*

"It's that Irish temper of yours," I said, brushing aside her question. "If you didn't still love him, you wouldn't be so angry at him for being a pigheaded ass." She sighed, and I added, "He deserves a chance to make it right, Cass."

A long silence passed, and I wondered if we had lost the connection. I almost asked "you still there?" when she said, "Why the altruism, Darv?"

"Can't a guy do a favor for a friend?"

"Not you. Not where Hagler and I are concerned."

"Then chock it up to good works so I get out of purgatory quicker." I listened to more silence and wondered if I'd taken the joke too far. Cass was very religious.

She took a sharp breath, and I couldn't help but think she was worried about me, which, at another time, I would have enjoyed. "What about you?" she asked. "Staying in the police bunkroom?" Before I could object, she added, "Hagler already told me about you and Pamela, so don't bother lying."

"Wouldn't think of it," I answered automatically. She snorted, and I knew it was her way of reminding me I had lied to her about being a cop for six months. "Don't worry about me. I'm on a stakeout, and my car's comfortable. Now, why don't you give Mel a call? He's planning on sleeping on one of the cadaver tables tonight. You know it'll kill his back."

"Funny," she said. "I'll think about it."

We said goodbye. I stared up at Pamela's upper-floor bedroom window. Maybe I saw a shadow duck behind floral-patterned curtains. I started my truck and pulled away.

51

Greenbrier Nursing Home

I n summer, night is a blanket that falls warm and inviting on Seattle, with the expectation of refreshing sleep and the anticipation of waking to a new day under the bright promise of the bluest skies in the world. Stir in the Cascades — Mount Rainier in particular, wearing a glimmering, hope-filled glacier — throwing glory upon the morning, and it makes getting through the night go faster.

I wasn't cheery as I drove into the Greenbrier Nursing Home's parking lot. More like I was a man on a fool's errand. *Seriously*, I told myself, *what do you expect to find? Evidence that a brain-dead patient is somehow able to kill victims with a mind trick that he absolutely needs a working brain to achieve?*

The alarm on my phone sounded at 8:00 pm, reminding me to take my Risperdal. I reached for the bottle but remembered I needed to refill the prescription. "Tomorrow," I promised myself.

Mine was the second car in the parking lot. Guess nursing homes didn't get a lot of visitors at night. Though, this was no ordinary nursing home. I once investigated a murder at a five-star hotel that didn't look as chic. Ornamental cherry trees lined a blue-stone walkway winding in gentle curves toward a marble-columned entrance of glass and stone. Stately Norfolk Island pines lofted fine blue needles above a recently mowed lawn. The online brochure stated the fees were $5,000 a week to lie in a coma with nurses looking after you 24/7. Chapman could afford it. I definitely wanted to die in a chic, top-of-the-line place like this one... after a long happy life.

The guard at the front door with the nametag Murray waved me through without checking my ID and went back to reading *Introduction to Security* by Fischer, Halibozek, and Walters. "Good luck with that," I said wryly. He nodded without looking up, proving the world is filled with obvious ironies nobody ever observes.

I strolled through the lobby — no cameras or sight lines from reception to the security desk at the entrance. I figured patients and their relatives' privacy was a selling point for the facility. It all told me Chapman could have wandered out of this place unnoticed, except for the trivial impediment of being in a permanent coma.

At reception, a gray-haired woman in blue scrubs with a stethoscope draped around her neck like she knew how to use it looked up from the computer she was studying. She forced a doleful smile of someone who knows you're here to pay last respects. "Visiting hours end at ten," she announced solemnly.

I flashed my badge. "I'm not here to say goodbye to a patient, Clara." It was the name on the tag pinned above her heart. "I'm following up on a couple of leads."

"Of course, lieutenant. Anything I can do to help."

"It's detective. What can you tell me about Myrna Toy?" I had listened to the missing person's report on my way over and didn't expect to find much other than that she had disappeared.

The nurse's eyes teared up. "I hope she's okay. I'd hate to think anything bad happened to her. She's such a dear."

"She ever do anything like this before — leave abruptly without a word to anyone?"

"Oh, no. She's been here all summer and is completely reliable and very much dedicated to the patients. Never missed a shift and even came in early so I could go home and see my Robert."

"Husband?"

"My cat, dear. He gets very lonely when I'm not home."

"The night she went missing, anything unusual happen?"

"Not while I was on duty."

So, maybe the niece tipped off Auntie Toy about something strange going on here, and Chapman took them both out while in his coma. Yeah, right. Still, he was my long shot and the other reason I was here. "What can you tell me about Andrew Chapman?"

"Very sad. His family just dumped him here, waiting for him to die."

"Isn't that what families do? I mean, it is a nursing home, and this isn't such a bad place to pass away."

She sniffed. "They never visit and never call except to ask if he's dead yet. They're not much of a family, if you ask me."

"He's in a persistent vegetative state, right?" I asked, careful to use the right terminology.

"Even coma patients can hear you, dear. If you don't believe me, you should talk to the nice nurse who reads to him every night. She's in his room right now." She flipped her computer screen toward me. Nurse Geneva Bowen sat at Chapman's bedside. "Room 124," Clara said helpfully.

My gut was telling me something fishy was going on between Bowen and Chapman. At the same time, my brain, cleared of Risperdal, put together connections on a level the normal human brain can't imagine. I reasoned that faking a vegetative state wouldn't be much of a problem for a man who had dedicated himself to understanding the human brain and its relationship to Earth's magnetic field and the astral plane. With the revenge-minded Bowen's help and the generous nonchalance of hawk-eyed Murray, escaping Greenbrier would be easy.

Satisfied the case had practically solved itself, I had already moved on to the more difficult part of proving my conclusion, when

Clara burst through my thinking. "You should ask Geneva about Myrna Toy."

"Why's that?" I managed to ask.

"The log shows she was here at the same time Myrna went missing."

"Thank you, Clara. You've been most helpful."

(Yeah, I'm thinking it, and you're thinking it — the plot has thickened. Now, don't you agree that clichés make the story go along much more smoothly than some flowery description of how my police senses, honed through years of solving murders, have come across a clue that tightens the web around Geneva Bowen and Andrew Chapman as accomplices to murder?)

I padded down the hall and stood quietly outside the closed door to 124. Maybe I'd hear something incriminating. After several minutes of listening to Bible verses I had memorized in Catholic school, I gave up and walked in without knocking.

52

Greenbrier Nursing Home

*M*ost *guilty people look the part, as if trying to hide something because they're new at the game of crime, their lawless acts impulsive. The professional criminal, on the other hand, knows he's run into a stretch of bad luck, like a downturn in the stock market, and he's looking for a better angle to climb back to even.*

Nurse Geneva Bowen acted as if holding a straight flush to my four of a kind. If she was connected to Myrna Toy's disappearance, I was never going to find the body. And forget any confession to helping the ghost killer. She stared at me with the same belligerent attitude she'd shown at the Harborview Medical Center's ER when we visited a couple of days ago.

"This is a private room," she said, voice glacial.

"I have a key," I said in the same tone and flashed my badge. I'd interviewed a few witnesses in hospitals and knew my way around the machinery — monitors for heartbeat, pulse, blood pressure. I even knew how a ventilator and an EEG operated. The ventilator softly pumped air into and out of Chapman's lungs. The EEG was a flat line on the screen. Brain dead. *But Chapman has the expertise to fake it*, I reminded myself.

I also thought of my mom and wondered if someday I'd be in a nursing home looking at a flat line on the screen in her room. Would I be able to pull the plug? Would I want to?

I cleared away the stray, spiraling thoughts and studied Chapman. He had the face Auntie Toy's diary described, down to the blue eyes, Roman nose, and bushy eyebrows. But the shrunken, cadaverous male lying on the hospital bed with tubes and wire leads sticking out of his body in every direction looked as threatening as a pail full of kittens, and I filed the suspicion he was faking a coma into the absurdities folder. So much for my real-world theory of the crime. I was back to the astral world's ghost killer.

I said, "I have some questions for Mr. Chapman."

The roll of nurse Geneva's eyes accused me of being the one in the coma. "He can't help you."

"Maybe you can."

"I have nothing to say to you."

"You can have nothing to say to me here or talk to me down at the station."

She laughed. "My brother's a cop. I know my rights. I don't have to go anywhere with you unless you have probable cause." She held up a Bible. "This look like probable cause?"

Fighting her was getting me nowhere, so I switched tactics. "You're right. I suppose I'm looking for justice."

"Damn straight, you should be. You should find the bastards who killed this man's family and left him for dead."

"Somebody has already done that," I said sympathetically.

"Then those bastards got what they deserved," she said without any self-incrimination.

"Yes, they did. But Auntie Toy didn't... nor her niece," I said softly, trying to wring some remorse out of Nurse Geneva's angry heart.

"Don't know anything about that," she answered in a voice smooth as silk and free of any conscience.

Out of the corner of my eye, I saw the EEG twitch a half step and lie flat again. I focused on Nurse Geneva. "Look, I couldn't care less if a gangbanger dies. One less skel on the street. But I don't like somebody doing my job and at the same time igniting a war in Chinatown that could hurt civilians. I take it personally when innocent people die."

She stood, and though she wasn't a big woman, she seemed to fill the space between the bed and me, blocking out the EEG monitor so I couldn't see if my words had any effect on Chapman. "I can't help you," she insisted. "I'm about to give Andrew a bath, so please leave and give us some privacy."

Nothing more legally to do here, so I left.

At the nurse's station, I stopped to ask Clara a few more questions. "What do you know about Mr. Chapman?"

"Only what I've read in the papers. He's a famous man."

"I know about his gay activism. I was wondering if there is anything unusual about him?"

She shook her head.

"What about here at the nursing home? Anything unusual happen since Chapman became a patient?"

"I've been the evening shift nurse for ten years here, and nothing unusual ever happens. Though..." She furled her lower lip with her teeth.

"What?" I asked.

"It's usually quiet, but in the last week, the lights have flickered and dimmed and flashed back on."

"What about the camera feeds to the patients' rooms."

Clara shook her head, then said, "Except for Mr. Chapman's room. His feed becomes staticky. You know, snowy."

Electromagnetic disturbances. "You check it out?" I asked, not sure whether I hoped Khoury was right or not.

"I went to his room personally. Everything was fine, just him lying in bed, and Nurse Bowen praying."

Of course she was. My gut told me something really hinky went on in that room. But my gut wasn't enough to convince Captain

Malvern or a judge. And what could I get a warrant for anyway, an ectoplasmic wiretap?

My brain, on the other hand, was now stoking the astral plane theory in spite of Chapman's EEG displaying a flat line, brain dead, persistent vegetative state. The unexpected twitch on the monitor had me wondering. That was a good thing about being off the Risperdal. All the walls were closing in, but they narrowed with the focus of a microscope that sharpened the perception of the problem on the horizon. If I let myself go off the drug long enough, I could see answers to questions the world hadn't even thought of yet.

I thanked Clara and headed toward the precinct and sleep. Once on the road, my drug-free subconscious had a mind of its own. I let it steer.

53

Northgate

Northgate is a neighborhood in north Seattle, between Puget Sound and Lake Washington. You can travel a few miles east or west and see water. It's named for the Northgate Mall, the first covered mall in the United States. You can look it up. It's a million square feet, two floors. And when I was growing up, it had this immense totem pole at the north entrance carved by a local architect. Now, the totem is at the Suquamish Clearwater Casino Resort. Mama worked at the mall as a cleaning woman for forty years. It's where she met Pops — at the food court.

Northgate. My subconscious took me to Khoury's home. I watched her front porch awhile, not sure my subconscious had any idea what it was doing, then decided, what the hell, go with it.

Her house was on 105th Street. About a mile down the hill, Puget Sound sparkled under a bright moon. I could have enjoyed the view for a long while, but the detective in me wanted to know why I chose here.

A light as bright as a mini-sun lit the two-bedroom bungalow's porch. I had to shield my eyes from the glow and wondered what she had to be afraid of and, maybe more importantly, why the neighbors didn't complain. I leaned on the buzzer.

Khoury pulled back a curtain in the window and did not look surprised to see me. She let me in, and we fell into each other's arms, our true feelings, repressed by my hostility toward her psychic bullshit, letting loose in a floodtide of passion...

Yeah, right. Let's skip the *bête noir* crime novel bullshit.

Sure, Khoury was beautiful; I was vulnerable because Pamela dumped me, and on some level, I realized from our first meeting that I found Khoury more than attractive. I'm a sucker for short, dark-haired women. If they know how to use a hammer, I want to marry them. Which was why I never proposed to Pamela. She couldn't use a hammer to break something.

Khoury went out of her way to make certain I would conclude that we would be hitting the sack together. She went into the kitchen to make coffee. I stayed in the living room and admired the artwork on her walls. Plaques beside each piece stated they were local artists, though I didn't recognize any of the names.

She was silent as a mouse nibbling at cheese in her kitchen, and I almost didn't hear her come into the room with a tray — two porcelain cups and a silver coffee server, which she explained were the only things she brought from Lebanon. They had belonged to her grandmother, and she couldn't bear to part with them.

She picked up her cup, and, no, she didn't gaze demurely at me over the rim. Taking a sip, she set it back down and asked bluntly, "Why are you here, detective?"

There were a lot of possible answers — I wanted to use her mystical abilities to tell me what I should do about Pamela and Cassandra... how to get the money to pay for my parents care... talk about Andrew Chapman. I said, "You're the psychic. You tell me."

"I don't need to be a psychic to know you're lost."

"What am I lost about?"

"Let's start with your eyes."

My eyes hadn't been darting around the room as if they expected something crazy to burst out of the walls and attack us, so I shrugged. "Nothing wrong with 'em."

"You have TD... tardive dyskinesia. Which means you're on a drug protocol either for schizophrenia, bipolar mania, or autism. I suspect the last, and you're afraid to let anyone know because you think it will affect your job."

Shit.

No, I didn't cuss aloud, though I'm sure my face showed my uneasiness at her spot-on description. It was a secret my parents never told anyone. Not even Liam McCrory knew. Forget about telling Pamela. And Cassandra wouldn't tell anyone.

As I said, I was spotted in first grade by Mrs. Baines after I solved all the jigsaw puzzles in the school instead of paying attention in reading class. Sure, I could read at three and played chess by four, beating everyone who came over to my parents' home until no one would play with me anymore. And no, I'm not a Magnus Carlson wannabe or a genius. Though, who knows? Maybe I would have become obsessed with chess if not for the teacher and Dr. Herschel's diagnosis and the Risperdal. I still followed the game, and I did jigsaw puzzles but not with the same single-minded, tireless focus I had at six when nothing else interested me. Maybe detective work is just a substitute.

No clichés could help me out of this no-win situation. And no denying it either. "Yeah," I said. "How long have you known?"

"Does it matter?"

"Professional interest. Plus, the little autistic guy inside my brain dedicated to the not-so-subtle art of counting things and who also likes to tell stories about what's going on around him..." I broke off, tried not to grin sheepishly at my fast talking, failed mostly, and finished lamely. "It helps him make sense of the world."

"From the moment we met," she said. "I have a cousin. His autism is much more severe. Drugs don't do anything for him."

I scrubbed my face with both hands. "Where do we go from here?"

"You didn't come here to confess your battle with autism."

"I just came from Greenbrier Nursing Home. Something hinky is going on there."

"Hinky?" she asked.

"Suspicious, like what's going on with you and your brother."

She pursed her lips. "My brother isn't hinky. He's complicated and overprotective of the family."

"He's protecting you?" I didn't get that vibe when I saw him. From the way he followed her around, I figured he was waiting for an opportune moment to catch her alone. Only, why he hadn't done so yet was the missing piece of this particular jigsaw puzzle.

"He's protecting the family," she said.

"From you," I said, because it was the obvious answer to why she'd uprooted from home and friends in Lebanon to come to the United States.

"We grew up in a small village where the oldest traditions have not yet caught up with twenty-first-century values. He thinks he's avenging my family's honor, since I refused the arranged marriage."

"You're kidding?"

She shook her head, the sadness in her eyes unmistakable.

And that was the last thing I saw before the flash-bang smashed through the window and exploded on the carpet. The next thing I knew, her brother, Mahir, had burst into the room holding a Glock-19 — the most popular handgun in America, cheaper than dirt, and the easiest to buy on the streets from your local unauthorized dealer.

The way he held it told me he knew how to use it, and by that, I meant he pointed the business end at us with the safety off and had undoubtedly chambered a bullet. He motioned me to toss my service weapon into the fireplace along with my back-up. Apparently, he'd seen his share of cop movies.

Mahir didn't play the part of a maniac. He acted and spoke like some kid here to deliver a Happy Meal with extra fries and a Coke. Okay, the Glock was a little over the top.

His sister wasn't intimidated at all. She blasted him with a spate of Lebanese, and I didn't have to speak the language to know she was telling her brother he was an idiot for coming here.

Mahir's reply was less obvious. I figured he was here to kill her, and I was collateral damage. Or maybe I was the reason, since she was an unmarried woman alone in her home with a man. Not that explanations for this kind of psycho bullshit ever help. We'd be dead whether we understood his motives or not.

And then a miracle, or more precisely, an out-of-the-frying-pan-into-the-fire calamity. The room darkened, then the lights came back on as bright as the sun. A lamp beside the fireplace exploded. All three of us stared at the broken fixture for a moment. Khoury and I ducked, knowing what was coming next. The rest of the lights burst in a sizzling torrent of glass everywhere. Several shards sliced Mahir's face.

"He's here!" Khoury exclaimed.

"You think?" I said as if the ghostly shadow hovering in front of the fireplace wasn't a dead giveaway. Yeah, I'm snarky even when scared.

Remorseless rage boiled out of the apparition, and I got a taste of what Fong, Chen, and Bennie Yee had felt staring into the glowing face of rampant death. Screw the psycho with the gun. In seconds, the ghost killer would drain my blood, and I could do nothing to stop it.

I guess I should have figured he'd make this play. After all, he went after Auntie Toy, tying up loose ends. The next person on his list had to be Khoury. She'd seen him. And, of course, in my zeal to solve this puzzle, I'd pulled the tiger's tail by visiting Greenbrier and confronting Nurse Bowen.

That was all the self-recrimination I had time for. A great weight pressed on my chest. I thought my heart was going to explode. Khoury fell to the floor, gasping. Her brother fired his Glock at the ghost. Jesus, those guns have a lot of bullets. One ricocheted and grazed my scalp. I slammed against the wall and slid to the floor, stunned. The pressure on my chest eased.

Mahir gurgled. Yeah, gurgled. It wasn't the noise a person makes when being choked. The sound coming out of his mouth was like a drain emptying. Draining the life out of a person, even on the astral plane, took a lot longer than I thought, a minute at least. The Glock slipped from Mahir's hands, and he collapsed to the floor, face and hands as white as a porcelain doll.

I tried to do something, but the pressure returned and pinned me to the rug. It felt like when you touch a live circuit. The weight on my chest increased, and I couldn't take a breath. Tiny meteorites shot through my vision, and I had the strange sensation bits of brain were leaking out of my head. Then I heard the same gurgling noise as from the brother coming out of my mouth, and I knew for certain what Auntie Toy had tried to warn me about — I was going to die.

My vision blurred, but I saw Khoury scramble out of the room. I had to time to bless fate that while the ghost killer killed me, she would escape. But she returned immediately, pointing a strange, pistol-like device at me. *How kind*, I thought. *She's going to put me out of the excruciating pain wracking my body.*

She pressed a button.

No noise, no bullets, just the raised hairs of static electricity during a thunderstorm over my skin. The effect was instantaneous. Whatever had been holding me was flung off, and I could breathe again. The ghostly shadow disappeared.

I tried to stand and didn't even make it to all fours.

54

Khoury's Home

*P**ops has another favorite saying. "Too soon old, too late smart." If this doesn't make any sense to you, you stand a good chance of never achieving either milestone.*

I almost didn't. I stirred and tried to get up.

Khoury held me down on the carpet with one hand. "Don't move," she cautioned. "You've lost a lot of blood."

I don't know what happened next. I must have passed out. When I came to, she was tending the scalp wound from the bullet with hydrogen peroxide and a suture kit.

"Your brother," I said, trying to sound sympathetic.

"Shush," she said. "You must conserve your strength. You nearly died." Maybe she knew I couldn't let it go. She frowned. "He was misguided. I will tell my parents he died saving my life, which is true in its own way."

"Lucky for me you stopped the ghost killer, or I would have joined him." I reached for my phone. "Got to call the police."

Khoury shook her head. "Forget it. Your phone won't work." She held up the weapon she'd used to stop the ghost killer — not a gun, but a half-gallon soda bottle with batteries and a couple of strange-looking gizmos duct-taped to the side.

"What is that thing?" I asked between gulps of air.

"A homemade EMP." She said it casually as if everyone had one on hand.

The blank look on my face told her I didn't have a clue what she was talking about.

"It stands for electromagnetic pulse."

I shrugged, and the blank look stayed in place, maybe due to the blood loss, but I didn't think so.

"Rapid invisible bursts of electromagnetic energy. You see them during lightning strikes. They can disrupt electronics they're aimed at." She showed me the weapon she'd constructed. Besides the batteries, the gizmos, she explained, were a voltage booster and a spark gap. A red button-switch replaced the cap. "Press the red button, and everything electronic within twenty feet is fried."

"You used the killer's electromagnetic power against him," I said, the light finally dawning inside my head.

She patted me on the shoulder like I was a prize student.

"I still need to call the police."

She went into the bedroom and returned with her phone. I called 911, identified myself, and gave the dispatcher my badge number. I also gave the color of the day. He told me black and whites were already on the way to my location. Next, I called Hagler, told him what and where and that we had another dead body. "Same as the others. This time, we have witnesses."

The calls drained me. Khoury helped me to a chair, because I insisted I didn't want to be lying on the floor when the police overran the place.

The next few hours passed like in one of those time-lapse videos. Police cars arrived. Hagler trotted up the steps behind them, took one look at me, and called for an ambulance. Once I was filled with IV fluids and a couple of pints of platelets, the EMTs decided not to transport me to the hospital — my service weapon might have had something to do with their decision. Mickey and Mack took the body away without cracking any Sasquatch jokes. Sheila Cummings did her forensic thing. Malvern arrived, chewing licorice non-stop — I think the fact the vic wasn't another I-5 Dragon or someone related to the tongs was the only reason he didn't take my badge; he said I could wait on the paperwork.

All at once, dawn arrived. The crime scene was abandoned except for yellow police tape and a rookie officer keeping neighbors away. Hagler, Khoury, and I sat in a back booth at Beth's Café away from the madding crowd of regulars and tourists clogging the counter. A twelve-egg omelet sounded good. We shared it while Khoury and I told Hagler what we experienced. I wanted someone else to hear it before I wrote a report that read like some nineteen-year-old stoner playing video games in his mama's basement.

Hagler never interrupted once. When we finished, he looked us both in the eyes, took a swig of coffee, and asked, "Supposing this is all true, how is it possible? I mean, how can the astral plane support this sort of thing?"

I turned to Khoury. "You're the ghost-hunting scientist."

Definitely not an American who would have talked through the meal while eating, Khoury put down her fork, took a sip of coffee, wiped her mouth with a cloth napkin (yeah, they use cloth napkins at Beth's), folded her hands in her lap, and told him what she knew.

"As a physicist, I've been recording astral plane phenomenon for a decade now. I've discovered the plane is powered by the Earth's magnetic field. In the last fifty years, it has been getting stronger because of the increasing amount of electromagnetic energy the world's power grids create."

Hagler shook his head. "How's that possible? Even the largest four hundred kilovolt lines put out a negligible electromagnetic field."

"True, but consider the immensity of the power grid in the US, Europe, Asia, South America, Middle East, Africa. All of that adds up and has augmented Earth's magnetic field, making it stronger. Before 2014, the Schumann resonance was 7.87 megahertz. By 2020, it more than doubled to 16.5."

"Is that supposed to mean something?" I asked in an effort to stay relevant in the conversation. Hagler and her were a couple of geniuses describing electrical engineering, and I was an autistic adult trying to solve a human/spiritual world jigsaw-murder puzzle. (That sounded a lot better in my head.) The loss of blood had somehow diminished my autism, as if it acted like Risperdal. Maybe the anemic tiredness that swept through me meant I didn't have enough energy to be consumed by the usual afflictions.

"The Schumann resonance is the resonance that taps into the astral plane," she explained. "The higher it goes, the more energy is available to people who travel on the plane."

After what happened to us last night, I believed her.

Hagler seemed to believe her too. "What about the dead guy?" He had his own report to fill out.

"My brother," Khoury said. "He was at my house to kill me."

Hagler looked at me.

I shrugged. "They weren't close."

"You know..." Hagler sighed, shook his head, and stared out the window at the street. Beth's morning takeout traffic was building in a line beside the cash register that snaked outside onto the sidewalk. Finally, he turned back to us and said, "I wouldn't believe any of this shit if you hadn't been nearly drained of blood yourself, Jack." He finished his coffee and got ready to leave. "You going to pick up the tab for this?"

William Chen's money was still in my pocket. "Sure."

When Hagler exited the place, I leveled my best detective stare at Khoury and asked, "You always carry one of those EMP weapons with you?"

"The spirit world is not always a friendly place," she answered.

"How did you know it would work?"

"I didn't, not for sure. But it takes a lot of electromagnetic energy to travel on the astral plane. I thought it was a good idea at the time."

"At least we have a way to stop the guy if tries again."

Her lips pursed in an I'm-not-so-sure kind of grimace.

"What? That EMP nearly fried him."

"The first time, yes. But he has the most powerful mind I've ever encountered in the astral realm. I'm sure he'll figure out a way to counter its effects by the next time we meet him."

Christ, I had to stop this guy, but from the way my body sagged against the booth's cushions, as if I were a boneless jellyfish, I couldn't take another bloodletting.

Nancy, our waitress, came by and refilled our coffees. I peeled off a hundred from the roll and told her to keep the change. When we were alone again, I said, "Why did you really leave Lebanon?"

"I told you. My family wanted me to marry, and I refused."

"You're leaving something out."

She let the air out of her lungs as if tired of holding in the truth. It certainly wasn't my winning personality or doggedness as a detective that broke her so easily.

"In Lebanon, I investigated the psychic phenomena happening in the region around my village. The older people grew afraid of me, said I had the evil eye. They begged me to stop. I was young, headstrong. They went to my parents. What could my father or mother do? I had refused to marry the man they chose for me. They went to the village elders. They knew my situation, so they went to the local Imam." She bit her lip.

"And?" I coaxed.

"He put a fatwa on my head."

"Christ," I whispered. "He ordered you killed because of your research?"

She took a sip of coffee as if it were normal for a priest to order someone killed when science clashed with orthodoxy.

"That's insane."

"Not in the Middle East, not in Muslim countries," she said sadly. "If a scientist's research doesn't conform to Islamic law and the

Koran, he is encouraged to correct himself. If he refuses, he will lose his position at whatever university he teaches. If he persists, he can lose his life."

"That's preposterous," I said.

She smiled at me as if indulging a child. "You're forgetting your own religious traditions. The Roman Catholic Church imprisoned Galileo for insisting Earth was not the center of the universe."

"Sure, but that was four hundred years ago. That kind of bullshit went out with the Scientific Revolution."

"In the West, yes. But in the Middle East, the traditions and teachings of Islam are still the most important fabric of everyday life." She sighed at the face I made. "Islam has a scientific history that stretches back to the eighth century. We brought advanced mathematics and astronomy to Europe's Middle Ages. We reawakened scientific inquiry to a world gone dark. We aren't barbarians. We are slow to catch up, is all."

"So, your brother wasn't really trying to uphold the family honor because you refused to marry your parents' choice."

"He was trying to cash in on the reward," she said, ashamed.

I'm glad I don't have siblings.

55

West Precinct

I've told you how beautiful Seattle is. It's distracting too. With so much going on in the Emerald City, in some ways, Seattle is the Royal Palace of Oz — a center for societies from all over the world... home to industry giants transforming the world's technological landscape faster than most users can dial tech support (if it weren't for a twenty-eight-year-old Millennial IT guy at the precinct, I couldn't keep up with the new shit coming out on my phone)... a combat zone in the culture wars.

But the Emerald City nickname comes not from Oz but from the evergreen trees within and surrounding the city, making it green year around. Of course, the trees don't hide the smog, the pollution, plastic bottle waste, or the homeless... a not-so-exclusive club of which I was now technically a member.

By rights, I should have been home resting. I was still a pint low by Hagler's estimate. But I couldn't do it. I had to solve the case — a must-see-it-through-to-the-end pressure in my autistic logic that made me set aside a little thing like severe blood loss.

Also, Pamela hadn't taken any of my calls. And I was pretty sure that even if I told her what had happened to me, when I swung by her house, my stuff would be scattered in the time-honored place of sidewalk and front lawn.

Sure, I could stay with my parents, but I didn't want to be that guy the rest of the squad snickered at, joked about his mom packing his lunch, or asked if he had a curfew.

Then there was Malvern. I told him my suspicions regarding Chapman and laid out the evidence Khoury's strange device showed and how she'd saved my ass with her homemade EMP gun. I wasn't so sure the latter impressed him.

I waited for the captain to take a bite of licorice and made my pitch. "We need to get a search warrant for the Greenbrier Nursing Home. At the very least, we have to tap the video feed to Chapman's room."

"Never going to happen," Malvern said stolidly.

"Boss, we gotta do this. It's our only chance to stop the ghost killer." (And yeah, after nearly being killed by that astral-psycho nut job, I was beyond caring what people called him.)

"Never going to happen," Malvern repeated as if that would make me shut up.

I still hadn't refilled my Risperdal prescription. Probably not a good idea, but the way my brain operated drug-free, I could see the answers to the murders as clearly as I could see the twists in the licorice candy Malvern was stuffing in his mouth at an alarming rate. It was like seeing the horizon up close for the first time in years. It felt glorious, though not manic. I mean, I knew for certain I could solve this puzzle as simply and quickly as any I had ever faced, and my voice got louder and shriller by the minute trying to convince him of the righteousness of my beliefs.

"You've got two eyewitnesses who can identify the killer," I insisted.

The captain held up his hand. I wasn't strung out enough to ignore it, so I grit my teeth and waited while impatiently making fists with my toes, since doing so with my fingers would have shown

Malvern something much more than could be attributed to anemia from blood loss was wrong with me. "What you have is a crazy-assed Arab shooting up his sister's house, who suddenly drops dead."

"He's Lebanese," I said, forgetting Malvern didn't appreciate glib remarks.

I'd never seen a grown man stuff so much candy in his mouth at one time. I swore he'd need an insulin pump just to survive the next fifteen minutes. After he stopped chewing and had wiped the sweat from his gleaming bald head with a blue bandana, he closed the door to his office. The squad always knew when Malvern was really pissed. First, the door closed.

He started off quiet, the proverbial calm before the storm, when the wind dies and insects are afraid to chirp. "Because you nearly died last night, I'm going to be kind, just this once. You've got bupkis. Let it go."

"My gut tells me I'm right, and you know it's never wrong," I said, ignoring the signs.

"No judge is going to issue a warrant on the supernatural craziness of your gut."

"Dr. Khoury's certain she can identify the killer with her EMF detector," I insisted.

Malvern grimaced, and the first muted puff of wind from the oncoming storm hit. "That goes double for a woman who claims to see ghosts."

"It's no claim. She can identify the killer."

Malvern's face darkened, becoming red as the licorice. "No judge in the world would admit her machine into a court of law. He'd be laughed off the bench and for good reason. There ain't no such thing as ghosts." His eyes narrowed, and he pointed a big beefy finger at me. "You of all people can't be serious about using her as evidence in a murder case."

"You told me to work with her, boss," I countered with what I thought was simple insouciance.

Malvern's eyes narrowed to nail heads, and the hurricane struck. "Get the hell out of my office. If I see you as much as pick up a pencil

250

between now and shift end, I will personally have you locked in a holding cell."

"On what charge?"

"Stupidity!" he yelled loudly enough to rattle the windows in his office.

Pops told me a long time ago that stupidity was *the* capital crime. The lack of Risperdal might have narrowed my thinking to a laser focus, but I was still smart enough to keep quiet when the storm was stronger than me.

I left the office as quickly as my enervated body would let me and did as I was told the rest of the day. My desk phone never rang, courtesy of my colleagues. By shift end, I was rested, not enough to chase down a perp, but enough to follow through with an idea I had stumbled upon thanks to my Risperdal-starved mind. Malvern would have labeled it anemic delirium. Maybe he would be proven right.

56

Greenbrier Nursing Home

I'll cut to the chase because no one likes a drawn-out ending, except in some weird fantasy universe, where it takes a page to describe the chair the hero is tied to and another page to describe the hat the fiend torturing him is wearing.

It's not what you think, or maybe you do know what's going to happen. I didn't, not at the time. It's all about being wrapped up in stopping a killer and not seeing the forest through the trees. Yeah, more clichés. But remember, they fill in the gaps, so things don't have to be explained. After all, I'm a detective not Toni Morrison.

Malvern was right. I had nothing any self-respecting judge would believe, let alone a jury would use to convict. That didn't mean I was out of options... illegal ones, anyway.

I called Hagler and told him to meet me at the precinct. I asked Khoury to come down too. She was going to be the wheelman this evening. Actually, if her claims about the EMF and EMP weren't exaggerations, she'd be doing the heavy lifting as well.

Khoury arrived first. She met me in the lobby. She wore a black headscarf and no makeup. She'd been crying, and I figured she had just delivered the news to her folks about their son's death.

"Thanks for coming down here, Zaina," I said. (Facing death together tends to put people on a first-name basis.)

"What's this idea of yours? You said it could make the case."

"Not here." I didn't want to take the chance Malvern could find out what I was planning and take me out of the game.

"My car's out front."

She helped me outside. I suppose I should have been in a wheel-chair. I was that weak. But I could move as long as I went slowly and didn't put too much strain on my heart. Even so, I rested at one of the stone benches near the entrance.

"Did you bring your gear?" I asked.

"It's in the car."

"Good." I took a deep breath. "That EMF device of yours... If you were near the killer, would it ping his energy signature. You know, tell us he's the guy?"

"Yes."

"Good." I was banking on a long shot, but what did I have to lose, other than my badge?

Hagler walked up. I told him my idea.

"Jesus, Jack. You trying to get us both fired, or killed?"

"You got a better way to find out who the killer is, Mel?" *Or stop him.* I didn't say that part out loud. I didn't want to clue these two in on my intentions. I had no qualms about being judge, jury, and executioner, but my conscience needed Khoury to confirm my suspicions before I went through with my plan. And because I had no idea how to build one of those handy EMP ghostbusters, I wanted Hagler along just in case.

Hagler shrugged. "Guess I don't have anything better to do."

I knew he was lying. His eyes were no longer red-rimmed and puffy, and he smiled for the first time in days, which meant he'd been talking to Cassandra, and they were patching things up. Hopefully after tonight, he'd still enjoy a long, happy life with her.

. . .

Carpe noctem. Seize the night.

No sense waiting around for the bad guy to show himself. By then, it would be too late. After last night, he knew what he was up against, and if he was as strong with the astral forces as Khoury suspected, I needed to stop him before he started. That meant going to his home turf — Greenbrier Nursing Home.

Standing in the facility's parking lot, Khoury activated her EMF. The antennas hummed loudly. She shivered. "He's definitely in this building," she announced after subjecting Hagler, me, and a pair of squirrels to thirty seconds of the device's eerie thrumming.

Ears ringing, I gave her a thumbs up.

"We have to hurry," she added, her mouth in a tight grimace.

"Why?" I asked.

"His energy signature is spiking. He'll be on the move soon."

I could be pretty sure he wouldn't be going after any I-5 Dragons. After last night, he was coming after Khoury and me.

Clara was on duty again. She recognized me, but I flashed my badge anyway. "We have urgent business with Mr. Chapman," I said.

Her hand reached for the phone. "Geneva Bowen warned me about you. I think you should leave before I call the police."

Ironic.

I didn't have a warrant, so I played my next best card. "This is the King County chief medical examiner, Dr. Hagler," I said and waited for Mel to show her his credentials. "It's imperative he sees Mr. Chapman immediately."

Nurse Clara bit her lip. She looked ready to tell us to go to hell, when the lights in the reception area dimmed. She glanced down at her computer screen. She didn't need to say anything. The strange look on her face told the story. I pulled the monitor around anyway. The camera in Chapman's room had gone to static.

Shit. We were too late. "Call the police," I yelled over my shoulder at Clara, for whatever good it would do, as we hurried down the corridor.

We burst through the door into Chapman's room. Actually, I hobbled. My heartbeat like a washing machine with an unbalanced load. Gasping for breath, I stared at a scene that scared me. In my years as a cop, I'd seen crazy and gory, but never anything as bizarrely abnormal as this.

Geneva Bowen, voice wailing like a revival preacher, recited Leviticus 24:20. "'And a man who injures his countryman, as he has done, so it shall be done to him, fracture for fracture, eye for eye, tooth for tooth.'"

As she prayed, a pale glow in the shape of a man climbed out of Chapman's body like a cicada splitting its shell. As the vaporous emanation emerged, it seemed to draw current from the lights and machines in the room, growing larger and brighter with each whoosh and slide of the ventilator until it stood rampant beneath an insane static that curled and arced around its human form in a lightning storm gone mad. Meanwhile, the EEG, which had been flat the night before, pinged dementedly in rhythm with the malevolent, pulsing glow of Chapman's astral body and Geneva's wailing prayer.

At its full height, Chapman's astral being straddled his physical self, dwarfing the shrunken ashen body. He stared at us, blue eyes blazing arcs of current. Tiny bolts of electricity circled his fingers. He was bigger, more powerful than last night. Waves of anger crashed through the room, each carrying a tidal roar of rage and the unmistakable plaint, "You must not stop me from avenging my family."

My hand went to my gun. Useless, I knew. Hagler's gasp froze in his throat, and he stared helplessly at the lightning-scribed ghost. Khoury was the only one who acted appropriately. She pulled the EMP from her pocket, but before she could aim it, the creature of light pounced. Khoury stiffened. Her arms flung out from her sides, transfixed as if she was being crucified on an invisible cross. Her face went pale, and that awful gurgling noise issued from her mouth.

The EMP slipped from her fingers and bounced off the floor and into my hands. I didn't know which end to aim. My hesitation gave Chapman the time he needed to shift from Khoury to me. The same pressure as before. The EMP fell onto the bed's pale white sheets. I crumpled onto the floor. Cold linoleum pressed against my face. "Hagler," I gasped.

Caught up in Chapman's deadly embrace, he too had fallen. His dark eyes stared into mine with the despair of a dying man.

Geneva Bowen prayed louder, all the while watching our agony with the fanatical passion of an Old Testament prophet wreaking retribution on her enemies.

As soon as Chapman released his deadly embrace, Khoury collapsed against the bed. The EMP lay in front of her. She grabbed the weapon but didn't aim it at Chapman. She went for the machines.

Geneva grabbed her from behind, pinning her arms to her sides. We were losing; I knew it, but Khoury didn't. She smashed the back of her head into Geneva's nose. Blood spurted crimson onto her scarf and dribbled down Geneva's lips and chin. The big nurse grunted but didn't let go. Khoury struck again; this time, Geneva fell, dazed, into her chair.

Khoury aimed the EMP and pressed the red button. The ventilator exploded in a shower of sparks. The hum of oxygen passing into Chapman's thin, corpse-like body stopped. The vitals monitor shuddered between gray static and green lines on black, while the EEG stuttered spastically from dead flat to hyperactivity.

The room went quiet. Chapman's ghostly self reared up as if he were choking. The pressure on my chest eased. My lungs labored to find enough oxygen to keep my heart and brain working.

The vengeful wraith spun and, spying his tormentor, fell upon her, engulfing Khoury in pulsing arms of bright light. She screamed and toppled backward onto Geneva Bowen's still form. Her face paled beneath Chapman's deadly embrace.

I tried to shout, but no sound came out of my mouth. I reached for Khoury, but my muscles refused to respond. Helpless, I listened to the breathless gurgle issuing from her throat like the sound of her soul being sucked from her body.

I gasped what was certain to be my last breath, when Chapman heaved upward like a drowning man clawing at the water's surface for air. Lightning tore through his aura. Moments later, it burst apart in a cannonade of sparks.

From somewhere, like out of a dream, Geneva Bowen screamed.

Khoury slid onto the floor. Her dark eyes glimmered under the room's pale light. I sighed, glad she had not paid the price for my gamble. Then the room went dark.

PART V

EPILOGUE

57

"The mind cannot live without the body. The body can't live without the mind," Hagler intoned. He sat in a chair by my bed at Swedish Hospital staring out the window at a distant, sun-speckled Elliot Bay. The TV was off; I didn't have the strength to turn it on, nor did I want it blaring into the room. I wanted sleep.

Hagler was as pale as a cue ball. I knew I looked worse. A second dose of Chapman's astral vampire powers had nearly killed me. A night and a day and another night in the hospital had helped, along with a couple of quarts of blood. As far as I knew, they threw red cells, white cells, plasma, and platelets at me, but I still felt more tired than I'd ever been — worse than being rode hard and hung up wet... beaten within an inch of my life... the living daylights knocked out of me... or any appropriate cliché.

"What are you going to do about Dr. Khoury?" he asked.

I shrugged.

"Jack, she killed Chapman and should be arrested."

"She saved our lives, Mel."

He sighed. "Who would believe it? Hell, I have a hard time believing it myself, and I was there." He shuddered, and both hands fluttered to his chest. "I was suffocating and couldn't do anything to stop it. Christ, Jack... I... I..." He trailed off.

"She saved our lives," I repeated doggedly.

"I suppose my autopsy will show Chapman died because the ventilator failed."

"And you can be sure the relatives won't bring a wrongful death suit. They'll be glad to get their hands on Chapman's money."

Hagler's face remained ashen, but he nodded.

"We may have a problem with Bowen," I said, recalling the lack of humanity in her eyes as Chapman sucked the life out of us.

He shook his head. "She's in the mental ward at Harborview. Apparently, Chapman's death sent her around the bend. She's claiming he was an avenging angel." Hagler paused and looked out the window.

I took the opportunity to ask, "You and Cassandra okay, Mel?"

"I'm going to the clinic with her."

"It's the right thing to do," I said. *The wrong thing for me*, I thought, biting my tongue, literally. I hadn't had Risperdal for several days, and my autism hammered at me to speak my mind. The only thing that kept me half normal was that the loss of blood had dampened my obsessive mania — I had already counted the number of spots in each of the ceiling tiles twice — and my hyper-activity — I slept most of the time. Once back on my feet, I would once more need the medication to function around others without drawing attention to my eccentricities.

Thankfully, Hagler changed the subject. "What will your report say, Jack?"

"When we got to his room, the ventilator failed, and Chapman died."

"Think Malvern will buy it?"

I could imagine the captain in his office reading the case file, a puzzled expression on his face, and a string of red licorice hanging out his mouth. "I think he's glad the mayor's off his back. No triad killings the past three nights, and Chinatown's business is picking up once more." Plus, I'd missed the opening day of the Chinook salmon run, which hurt worse than a suspension without pay ever could have. It was enough for him to leave me alone.

Hagler shook my hand. I didn't try to sit up. I was still weak, and the doctor's orders were to refrain from activity. Too much strain on my heart. If I rested, I'd be back at work in a couple of weeks.

He looked past me and waved. Khoury stood in the doorway. Her black head scarf had been replaced by a paisley one, the floral reds matching her lipstick. She wore eye shadow too, which gave her pallid complexion a haunting look of beauty.

Her appearance wasn't lost on Hagler. He grinned at me and leaned close, whispering, "What are you going to do about her?"

"Why?" I asked, suspicious of his concern.

"She saved your life, twice. Now she's responsible for you."

"That's a Chinese custom, Mel. Among Muslims, it's kismet... destiny."

"There you go," he said, laughing. He left, whispering in her ear as he passed. She patted his arm. They exchanged smiles.

"What brings you here, Zaina?" I asked when she came over.

She squeezed my hand. "Wanted to make certain you were okay, Jack."

Yeah, facing death together definitely puts you on a first-name basis. "Doctors say I'll be good as new by the end of the week."

"You missed the opening of salmon season."

"You've been talking to Liam."

"A very interesting man with a bright future."

"We're going out next weekend. You should come along."

"Maybe next time." She smiled.

Paranoia at all the smiling spread through me, and I gripped the sheets, pulling them tighter toward my chin. "What's the smile about?" I asked cautiously.

"The future is not what you think it is."

"Between you and me?"

She answered with another smile, then said, "I brought you something." She reached into her coat pocket and pulled out a plain brown bag. She opened it and showed me the contents.

"Thanks," I said.

She opened the bottle and gave me a tab of Risperdal. She helped with the water, too, holding the straw for me. We talked about inconsequential things until the nurse came in and shooed her away. "Mr. Doyle needs his rest."

"I'll be back tomorrow," Khoury said.

"I'd like that."

She left, and the nurse smiled at me. "A man in your condition shouldn't be excited by his girlfriend."

"She's not my girlfriend," I said.

"Uh-huh." The nurse winked and left me with a whole lot of time on my hands to wonder what everyone was smiling about. I fell asleep before I could come up with any answers.

58

S wedish Hospital discharged me when I could sit up and take nourishment with utensils instead of a straw. McCrory texted me pictures of the record fish he and Malvern had caught.

I had a couple of weeks before I could officially go back to work. I spent some of the time driving around aimlessly, though very happy to be alive, until I found myself parked outside Cassandra's home. Hagler's car was in the driveway. They were back together. I moped between gloom and happiness.

Life interrupted my pity party with a phone call from Pamela. Last time we had been in the same bed together, I had thought of her as a shrew. It was unkind and was the lack of Risperdal speaking... mostly. For some time, our relationship had been running on fumes. Living on charity from a lover wasn't my style.

I pressed decline and texted her that I would be by for my things in a couple of days. She could leave them in the driveway for now. Seattle's rainy season was still a few days away, thanks to global warming.

I drove away from Cassandra, too. I went to my parents' home, where I met with the home care specialist who would be the lead person taking care of them. Luis had switched from King County's program to the private sector — more benefits, better pay. It was a relief to know Mama and Pops had a great person taking care of them. Paying for it all was still a problem, but I'd cross that bridge when the first bill arrived.

I had no place to go. Then Uncle Lo invited me to his office. He'd come to visit me in the hospital. Rare for the old man to leave the restaurant. It was nearly noon on a Friday, and Chinatown was packed with tourists and businesspeople now that it was safe to visit again. Finding a place to park should have been impossible. But outside the Good Luck Noodle Shop, a waiter held open a spot for me.

I tipped him a twenty. Maybe too much, but I hadn't relished the thought of walking several blocks from and to my car. I was out of danger but still weak.

The noodle shop was crowded, every table and stool at the counter filled. Uncle Lo's booth was empty. As soon as I sat down, the old man came out, playing the part of the nineteenth-century merchant with gusto — robes, brocaded hat, jewel sheaths on his little fingers. On his arm was a pretty Chinese-American woman, probably mid-twenties. "My grandniece, Myrna... Myrna Toy." He introduced her without a hint of relief in his voice. "I wanted you to know she was fine."

She held out her hand; we shook. She blushed and fled into the kitchen.

"You knew all along she was all right the night you called me about her disappearance," I said.

He didn't deny it. He didn't apologize either. "You needed a push in the right direction."

We talked about my health, which he was happy to hear was improving. He had special food and a large mug of tea brought to the table.

"To re-invigorate your *chi*," he explained, pushing the brackish liquid toward me.

The tea smelled like canal water, but the aroma of the food was superb.

"Heard the I-5 Dragons decided to leave Chinatown," I said.

Uncle Lo smiled, his gold front tooth gleaming at me as if it held a secret. "Blind Tseng very kindly offered them a feng shui reading for a very reasonable price." He shook his head gravely. "It was very bad for them. They'd never have prosperity as long as they occupied the building."

"I don't suppose the coincidence that Tseng is one of your astrologers was a concern to the triad?" I asked dryly.

"He is an honorable young man, just like his father before him. Their family has a long history, many generations of telling fortunes and guiding people to prosperity," Lo said sagely. "You should listen to him. I can set up an appointment for you."

"I'll pass, Uncle Lo, but thanks."

He clapped his hands, and his nephew appeared. Malcolm was no longer dressed in Western blue jeans, T-shirt, and a backwards baseball cap. He wore a traditional tai chi uniform with soft crepe-soled shoes. His hair was once more black and combed neatly on his head. He carried a small chest with a paper bag on top of it. He set both in front of Uncle Lo, bowed, and vanished back into the kitchen.

"Malcolm going into the family business?" I asked.

"He is a dutiful young man." Lo picked up the plain brown paper bag and handed it to me. "More of the herbs to invigorate your *chi*," he said. "Drink it twice a day."

The tea tasted like something a frog would spit up, but I would drink it. Lo had the best acupuncturists and herbalists in his employ. His third wife, fifty years younger than him, just had a baby boy. I set the bag next to me. My eyes were riveted on the chest. Rosewood sides, gilded lid. I knew what was inside — ten smuggler bars of gold.

"For you and your brothers in the police force," Lo said. By brothers, he was referring to the Police Tong, of course.

I thanked him. It wasn't a gift I could refuse. Nor could I just pocket it for myself to pay for my parents' care.

We spoke some more, and he was called away. I left with the chest. The nephew carried it out to the car for me. I didn't worry about being robbed. All the tongs were grateful the murders had stopped, with the added benefit that the I-5 Dragons had left Seattle.

59

The afternoon flew by. I arranged for the Police Brotherhood's accountant, Leung Po, to take the chest off my hands. It would disappear into the tong's Cayman accounts to be used to open a recreation center for disadvantaged kids in Tukwila, a city just south of Seattle on the way to SeaTac Airport. It ranked as the most dangerous town in Washington and the second-worst place to live. They could use something to keep the kids out of trouble and make police work less hazardous.

Evening arrived, and I eventually found myself at my desk in the West Precinct. If this narrative sounds tired, it's because I was tired and still had no place to sleep. I was grateful to be back on the Risperdal. It beat my unmedicated state. Several times at the hospital, I wanted to throttle the doctors and nurses because I thought they were trying to kill me. Good thing the bloodletting left me as weak as Starbucks coffee.

I checked my desk as I always do before I left for the day. The squad liked to play practical jokes on me. The bottom drawer was hard to open, and I prepared for a take on the classic snakes-in-a-Pringles-can prank. Instead, I found a bulky manila envelope that had caught on the top. Forcing the drawer open ripped the corner. I peered inside.

Hundred-dollar bills... lots of them... maybe a couple of thousand. Enough to cover my parents' expenses for at least two years. My stomach had that clenched feeling when you're pulled to safety from certain death. That reaction passed, and wariness set in. Who had gifted me the money?

I inspected the envelope. A tiny chop, the kind used by Chinese businessmen as a signature, was stamped in the upper right-hand corner. I pulled out a magnifying glass (yeah, I'm a regular Sherlock Holmes) and examined the seal. It was elegant, the ideogram even more exquisite because of its minute size. Whoever had done this was an artisan who appreciated fine craftsmanship. Someone like Uncle Lo.

I sighed. *Guanxi...* We were even until the next time one of us needed help.

Malvern dropped by while I was deciding what to do about the unorthodox payment for ending the killer ghost. He spied the open desk drawer. "Still looking for the gecko the squad put there last year?"

I nodded, afraid to speak.

He sat down in the chair opposite me. "You're back too soon, Doyle."

I found my voice. "I'm not staying."

"I read your report, and Hagler's." He paused, giving me a chance to explain.

I shrugged. Sure, it read like Mary Shelley's *Frankenstein* novel, but it was the truth.

He pointed at my hands. "What you got there?"

I realized I was still clutching the envelope. Maybe I should have shown Malvern the money. On the other hand, how would I explain the Chinese custom of *guanxi* to someone who didn't have a Twitter handle and thought Facebook was a binder full of mugshots. I said, "Filthy ME porn Hagler sent me."

Malvern rolled his eyes. "I'll be so glad to be rid of this job." He stood wearily, put the end of a red vine in his mouth, paused, pulled it out and stared at the crimson licorice as if it were poison. He dropped the offending candy into the wastebasket beside my desk. "I have three months left to retirement. You know what I could use most at this moment? A cigarette and a shot of tequila."

Right now, retirement would be a blessing. I said, "Who's going to be your replacement?"

The captain snorted. "I should pay you back for all the ulcers by recommending you for the job."

I didn't laugh. My gut told me he meant it.

"Go home, Doyle," he said. "That's an order." Malvern walked out.

I was left holding the bag.

ABOUT THE AUTHOR

Mark Reeder writes science fiction and fantasy for both adults and young adults, and is the author of the Jack Doyle paranormal detective series. He's kicked around the universe long enough to have more than a few bumps and bruises. Roughed up and battered like his hat, he's still looking for the exit.

AFTERWORD

Go to hangaripublishing.com to learn more about the Authors and stay up to date with their newest releases.